SACRED SPACES

SACRED SPACES

Contemporary Religious Architecture | James Pallister

Φ

CONTEMPORARY RELIGIOUS ARCHITECTURE

God, death and eternal life: of life's many existential questions, they don't get much bigger than these. With this in mind, it's easy to see why, for many architects, the opportunity to tackle these themes when commissioned to design a major religious building comes as a defining moment of their careers. [1] Great architecture requires not just a good architect, but a good idea, and a good client. Religion's inquiry of humanity and beyond ensures plenty of fertile ground to generate strong ideas, and the position which religions have often held – close to both political and economic power – makes for clients, or a body of commissioners, willing to dig deep to provide the requisite financing.

This book is a global survey of some of the best religious architecture of the last ten years. Mosques, synagogues, churches, cathedrals, chapels, temples: this publication takes in all of the prominent world faiths, and spans the western and eastern hemispheres, from a Christian church on a sacred Chinese mountain and a conservative Jewish community centre a stone's throw from the Golden Gate Bridge in San Francisco to a mosque in Sudan and a Buddhist meditation centre in The Netherlands. As the critic and architect Robert A. M. Stern has written, 'Historically the religious building type has often been the locus for advancement and invention in architectural design.' [2] Great architects have produced some of their best work in the services of religion: for example, Andrea Palladio at San Giorgio Maggiore in Venice, Le Corbusier's La Tourette Monastery in France, and Basil Spence's Coventry Cathedral in England are just a small sample of the rich lineage of religious architecture. The buildings featured in this book are testament to the inspiration that religious buildings continue to offer to a new generation of architectural talent.

This set of thirty projects from around the world – from the USA and countries across Europe, to Japan, China, Taiwan, Mexico, Sudan and beyond – show the ways in which contemporary architects are exploring new methods of constructing religious buildings, developing centuries-old typologies and creating new ones. The development of

1
Edwin Heathcote and Laura Moffat, *Contemporary Church Architecture*, Wiley, 2007

2
Karla Britton (ed.), *Constructing the Ineffable. Contemporary Sacred Architecture*, Yale University Press, 2011

→
The city of Coventry in England has had three cathedrals. The first was St. Mary's, of which only ruins remain, the second a 14th-century Gothic Cathedral, that was ruined after being bombed during World War II, and the third St Michael's Cathedral – a celebration of 20th-century architecture designed by Basil Spence and completed in 1962.

contemporary architecture has long been a story of borrowing and adaptation, and ideas flow across porous borders: just as religions have developed from, and added to, specific cultural traditions as they move from place to place. Consequently the geographic scope of the book takes in every habitable continent on earth, with architecture from North and South America, Europe, Africa, Asia and Australasia.

This essay introduces some of the projects and themes dealt with in the book and outlines what is here meant by 'religious' and 'sacred' architecture. Common characteristics of sacred architecture shared by several faiths are identified, and the way in which the recent history of contemporary architecture has coalesced with shifting trends within contemporary religion is explored. There will be an attempt to outline some trends in contemporary religious architecture and, finally, a look to the future. It can be argued that, far from being on the decline, religion is on the rise, and is increasingly becoming a catalyst for change in contemporary society. The buildings within these pages are both evidence of, and a means of expressing this, and develop the ways in which we articulate and experience sacred spaces in our world today.

What, however, is meant by the term 'religious buildings', or 'sacred spaces'? A straightforward antonym to the sacred is the profane, that which pertains to the worldly, the everyday. The term 'religious building' is perhaps a more specific, and therefore useful, term, as it roots the meaning in something more precise. The nineteenth-century French sociologist and philosopher Émile Durkheim (1858–1917) brought the two terms – religious and sacred – together in his explanation of religion, defining it as 'a unified system of beliefs and practices relative to sacred things, that is, things set apart and forbidden – beliefs and practices which unite in one single moral community called a Church, all those who adhere to them'. [3] While Durkheim's use of the word 'Church' draws attention to his bias towards the dominant religions of his day, namely Christianity, his definition is

3
Émile Durkheim, *The Elementary Forms of the Religious Life*, Book 1, Ch. 1, Allen & Unwin, 1915

←
Hagia Sophia, in Istanbul, Turkey (537–1453) started life as a Greek Orthodox basilica, was briefly in use as a Roman Catholic cathedral before being transformed into an imperial mosque in 1453. In 1931 it was secularised and turned into a museum.

→
The chapel of Notre Dame du Haut, designed by Le Corbusier (1955) – a prime example of what the architect referred to as 'ineffable space'.

broad enough to be applicable to faiths such as Buddhism or Japanese Shintoism, whose practitioners may not include a 'god' in their belief schema, nor identify as being religious as such, rather are practices, or ways of being. For Durkheim, the explicit reference to a belief in the supernatural or divine was not needed in his definition. It would be anachronistic, for example, to attribute a belief in the supernatural to medieval man, as the division between that which can be explained rationally (as natural), and that which cannot, only came into existence with the advent of the Enlightenment in the seventeenth century and the development of scientific methodology.

For later scholars of religion, Durkheim's explanation wasn't sufficient; a modern definition of religion had to include an explicit belief in the supernatural. This serves to address what might be called the 'football fan' or 'boy scout' problem: diehard sectors within these groups may well have a unified system of beliefs complete with their own 'sacred' paraphernalia (the pitch, the campfire) yet are plainly not religions. Similarly, a church may find itself to be very similar to a library once we take away its reference to the divine. Both comprise a generous space in which transcendental activity may well take place, for a specific community, where there are shared norms, taboos, expected forms of behaviour and a clear hierarchy and priesthood, whether they be bespectacled librarians or cassock-wearing monks. All the buildings in this collection are united by a belief that they offer some means of touching, or making contact with, a divine or supernatural power. Of course this belief in contact with the transcendent will not be universally held by all who visit, or indeed by those who design these buildings, but it is important to the core of the communities they serve. The idea of touching and being touched by the divine is a thread that runs through all of the buildings in this book. There will be much discord between the specific practices of the different religions represented – Buddhists may quarrel with the monotheism of Christians, Muslims find no attraction in the heavy use of Buddhist pictorial representation, Catholics find the lack of formal priesthood in Islam

hard to fathom, and Calvinists (1887–1965) who conform to Protestant traditions) tut disapprovingly at the lavish places of worship some Catholics frequent. Yet it can be said that, even with all these considerable differences taken into account, the thread which binds these institutions and these buildings, is stronger than any that separates them.

Having seen what the buildings in this book are united by, it is worth exploring whether there is a common means of expressing a desire to connect with the divine. What is it that characterizes transcendental space? Here, borrowing a phrase of the Swiss-French Modernist master architect Le Corbusier may be useful. Although he didn't identify with a specific religion – William J. R. Curtis recorded Le Corbusier as saying, when questioned about religion at La Tourette (the monastery he completed for a Dominican order near Lyon in France) in 1961, 'I have not known the miracle of faith'. Le Corbusier was nonetheless very much interested in matters spiritual and metaphysical. [4] What he did claim to know was 'the miracle of ineffable space, the consummation of plastic emotion'. This rather lofty language, referring to *l'espace indicible'* or 'ineffable space', describes space with a quality so powerful that it cannot be put into words. For Le Corbusier this occurred when 'work reaches a maximum of intensity, when it has been made with the best quality of execution, when it has reached perfection … When this happens the places start to radiate. They radiate in a physical way and determine what I call 'ineffable space', that is to say, a space that does not depend on dimensions but on the quality of its perfection. It belongs to the dominion of the ineffable, of that which cannot be said.' [5]

Le Corbusier was not referring exclusively to religious architecture; *l'espace indicible* could also be found in humdrum, profane types of buildings: office blocks, houses, schools and so on. However, it is fair to say that while ineffable space is not unique to religious buildings, most religious buildings will aspire to articulate or inspire in the visitor some element of 'that which cannot be said'. So it can be argued that Le Corbusier's idea of

4
William JR Curtis, *Le Corbusier, Ideas and Forms*, (Phaidon, 1986), 179

5
Quoted from Karla Britton in *Constructing the Ineffable. Contemporary Sacred Architecture.*

ineffable space becomes a useful term for the elements, or qualities that are required to make great religious architecture. It is the element that goes beyond the needs of programme and function – expressions of ritual, hierarchy, and doctrinal requirements that the religious building must also fulfil. It becomes a phrase, in effect, to describe the indescribable.

The complexity of subjects that religious architecture confronts has meant that it has long been a vector for many different styles and means of architectural expression. The domes of the Hagia Sofia in Istanbul expressed mathematical sophistication and power; great Norman cathedrals such as Durham Cathedral articulated the fortress-like power of the church; the grand facades, flying buttresses and delicate tracery of Gothic cathedrals like Notre Dame in Paris expressed an uplifting to the heavens to impress the medieval pilgrim; today minimalist detailing and stripped-back chapels help to articulate the quietude and peace some seek in religion. Though long associated with clearly drawn typologies that grew out of doctrinal prescription – the cruciform-plan church, the square mosque, the rectangular synagogue – religious subjects offer a surprisingly broad range of expression for architects.

This having been noted, we can identify shared themes and characteristics across contemporary and historic sacred spaces. Accordingly, these give this book structure, breaking it into five sections, each with a different theme: congregation, clarity, mass, reflection and revelation.

The first chapter, Congregation, looks at the common fundamental requirement of many faith buildings to gather together a group of people to worship as one body. Whether this is the community-built timber simplicity of the Kärsämäki Church in Finland (page 28), or the semi-temporary Cardboard Cathedral by Shigeru Ban in New Zealand (page 22), these

buildings all remind us that though the architecture may bedazzle, inspire, or perhaps even subdue, what brings them to life is their inhabitants – before the church, comes the people. This basic requirement of uniting a congregation in a room is addressed by the most straightforward religious typology: the temple. It is the temple from which both mosque and church typologies developed and is a form that remains a common typology in Japan and China, and which is common to most religious buildings. The temple offers probably the most basic architectural form for worship, echoing the primitive hut.

The second chapter, Clarity, explores how a constant spiritual leitmotif across many religions over many centuries – that of paring back to essentials, of self-denial, and of purity – has found an attractive formal articulation in early twenty-first-century Minimalism, whether that be in the St Moritz Church by John Pawson in the Bavarian city of Augsburg (page 74), or Chandgaon Mosque in Bangladesh (page 68).

More than a century and a half ago, in the 1850s, the German critic and art historian Gottfried Semper (1803–1879) wrote of the 'building of man' and of the 'building of the earth', and the area in between, in which architecture was created. He distinguished the tectonic – associated with lightweight, linear components – from the stereotomic, which described a form of heavy earthwork construction. The stereotomic was an extension of the earth, which would provide the base for the tectonic, and it is the transition between the tectonic and stereotomic where architecture comes into being. [6] Building on Semper here, it could be argued that it is in the tension between solidity and lightness that ineffable space is created; chapter three, Mass, deals with this balancing act.

It should be noted that the purpose of many of the buildings in this book is to help people deal with the prospect and reality of death. Indeed, questions of mortality and posterity are never very far from architecture, and particularly religious architecture. Most buildings

6
Gottfried Semper, *Style in the Technical and Tectonic Arts; or, Practical Aesthetics*, Getty Research Institute, 2004

←
Joseph Paxton's Crystal Palace (1851) erected to house the Great Exhibition. The enormous open spans achieved in this cast-iron and plate-glass building, an extraordinary structural and technical feat for its age, meant that religious buildings lost their monopoly on awe-inspiring architectural spaces.

→
A Free Presbyterian Church in the Isle of Skye, Scotland exemplifies a simple, classic church with its white-washed walls and pitched roof.

→ →
Religious building as the embodiment of architectural advancement – the celebrated Chiesa del Santissimo Redentore (1592), Venice, Italy which is considered by many to be the crowning achievement of architect Andrea Palladio's career.

are expected to outlive their creators, but religious buildings offer their architects, clients, users and visitors the prospect of immortality in a way that few others do. Buildings of permanence and history – those that have hosted generation upon generation of people – help make more tangible a conceptual timescale that is incredibly difficult to grasp for those with a belief in an afterlife.

This engagement with death can be articulated in a strict programmatic sense, such as at the Rituals Crematorium by +udeb arquitectos in Colombia (page 114), or in a more general sense, in a community synagogue such as the Beth Sholom synagogue in San Francisco, USA (page 108), where funeral rites make up just one aspect of community life that its congregation share. The permanence of buildings can offer both primal reassurance of continuity in their long-lasting bricks and mortar, or equally, a comparative reminder of the fragility and impermanence of human life: 'ashes to ashes, dust to dust'. [7]

7
Burial service phrase from the Anglican *Book of Common Prayer.*

Chapter four, Reflection, deals with spaces of quietude, reflection and peace, including the Taiwanese Water-Moon Monastery for Buddhist monks (page 160) and the Islamic Cemetery for Muslims in Austria (page 148), the country's first state-run Islamic cemetery, a well-resolved piece of architecture and a model of how enlightened multiculturalism works at its best.

Chapter five looks at the complex idea of divine revelation and the architecture that attempts to facilitate this direct religious experience. Some religious believers attempt time-consuming and grueling excursions to achieve this revelation, like those pilgrims trudging through the baking summer sun en route to the adoration of the Virgin of Talpa in Mexico that Luis Aldrete's Pilgrim Route Shelters (page 202) cater for. The last two hundred years have seen many societal changes with which both religion and architecture

have been deeply involved. The biggest challenge for the architect of religious spaces today is that developments in technology, especially in the western world, have effectively removed the monopoly over sacred spaces that the church once had. Before the nineteenth century, awe-inspiring spaces were the preserve of rulers and religions, and most of those that were publicly accessible would have been religious spaces. One could argue that the development of the cast iron column did to sacred architecture what the printing press did to the Catholic Church in the fifteenth century. Once the wide spans and vaulting ceilings, formerly the near-exclusive preserve of cathedrals, became affordable without the large expense of human labour, and became commonplace in the building of factories, railway stations and libraries, the religious architect encountered a dilemma. Since the palace, the shopping malls, the office atrium, and that great transcendent space of our time – the art gallery – have eroded the monopoly that religion once had, where does the architect go? The answer is usually to create regionally appropriate mediations between the latest architectural thinking and the (usually even-slower moving) demands of the religion in question. Of course, just as the reformation was not solely attributable to the invention of the printing press, many more factors play into the more complex challenge faced by architects of contemporary religious buildings.

These factors – some of which are recent challenges, while others have roots as far back as the Renaissance – can broadly be bundled together as: the rise in individualism; the development of the scientific method; more widespread access to education; and the shrinking of the world brought by the increased speed and decreased cost of travel. All these factors were – as early as Durkheim's day – expected by many to see religiosity decline, and ultimately disappear, an atavistic irrelevance in a modern world. This idea has been called the secularization thesis. But this notion cannot be further from the truth. Religiosity is as influential as ever with research from the Pew Research Center's Forum on Religion & Public Life, an American think tank that provides information on social issues,

public opinion, and demographic trends, suggesting that eight out of ten of the world's six billion population is affiliated with a religion and the very modernity that was supposed to eradicate religion has merely allowed new, interesting religious hybrids to flourish. [8]

Similarly, within architecture, though there may now be familiarly designed skyscrapers in many cities of the world, the 1930s utopia of a universal Modernism sweeping the world has been seen to be exactly that, a utopia; regional cultural differences in building, programme, topography and climate are still incredibly important, especially away from the central business districts, in the fine grain of towns and cities. Cross-pollination happens more quickly than it ever has, but generally, as Tzonis and Lefraivre have noted, this sharing of ideas leads to hybridity and pluralism rather than homogeneity. [9]

Though the secularization thesis can be rebuffed, it is fair to say that something has changed – not that we have all become secular but that religions have in their own way become somewhat secularized. Rather than suffusing all areas of someone's life, religion becomes compartmentalized. The flip side to the breaking down of the societal bonds that once strengthened religion can, paradoxically, directly aid it: individual identity, of which religion can be a powerful component, becomes ever more important. For Austrian-born American sociologist Peter Berger (1929–), secularization is at work within religion, as it becomes part of an 'individual's search for a personal religious preference'. [10] Eminent Islamic and Middle Eastern studies writer Malise Ruthven predicts that Islam will continue to develop along more secular lines, with faith becoming more of a private part of identity, rather than a publicly defining one. [11]

Over the last thirty years western democracies have seen once-predictable, class-based voting shift to much more individualized decision-making. As mass political ideologies have fallen, individual identity politics have been ascendant. Religion has

8
The Pew Research Centre's Religion & Public Life Project www.pewforum.org
9
Alexander Tzonis & Liane Lefaivre: 'The Grid and the Pathway', *Architecture in Greece*, 1981
10
Malise Ruthven, *Islam: A Very Short Introduction*, New York: Oxford University Press, 2000.
11
Tzonis & Lefaivre: 'The Grid and the Pathway', *Architecture in Greece*, 1981
12
Samuel P Huntington, *The Clash of Civilisations and the Remaking of World Order*, New York: Simon & Schuster, 1996

←
The Cardboard Cathedral by Shigeru Ban (2013) is a contemporary example of the importance of 'one central room'. A single shared space is common to the origins of almost all religions – a place for gathering, for contemplation and for prayer.

→
In February 2010, Tom Greenall and Jordan Hodgson were commissioned by the writer and philosopher Alain de Botton to collaborate on the Temple for Atheists. The temple, designed to stand in the City of London, is just one of a number of contemporary projects that take secular spaces of worship seriously.

been intertwined with what we may now call personal reinvention for millennia, and contemporary tendencies only reinforce this process. Religion can offer stability and control in one's life when it feels that there is little – a situation faced by many thanks to some of the rapid changes brought about through globalization and the liberalization of the labour market associated with the now hegemonic neo-liberal political and economic policy. One does not need to be a fully paid-up subscriber to Samuel Huntington's *Clash of Civilisations* thesis to see that religion is still enormously important to geo-politics, from the Blair-Bush axis of foreign intervention, of which religious fervour appeared to be part, to Sunni and Shia feuds in Iraq, bringing Iran back into the international community. Christianity may be lampooned as weak and ineffectual in northern Europe but it is flourishing in Africa and Latin America. The UK's trade deficit has its parallel in religiosity, whence it once sent missionaries, now it receives. [12]

All this makes for exciting times in religious architecture. One of the trends that can be noted in this book is that in many cases religious buildings are becoming more and more alike. The combination of an increased social informality, need for flexible space, and – in the Roman Catholic's case of the Second Vatican Council – doctrinal changes, have seen Christian churches move away from the cruciform format and back to the 'large room' model, often used in Islamic places of worship. Typologically, it could be said that the temple, as opposed to the church, is in resurgence. The one-off building and the complex – Peter Zumthor's chapel in Germany versus the Kuokkala Church in Finland, for example – continue to be two important types, yet societal shifts and diverse urban communities mean that the complex is more likely to cater to a self-selected group than those from a given area: the parish has given over to the club.

Within these complexes the delineation of sacred and non-sacred space is normally very clear, continuing a trend towards the specialization of space that began in the Victorian

←

The 'other' sacred space in contemporary society – the art gallery, especially in its form as 'white cube' such as this example of the New Museum of Contemporary Art, New York, by SANAA – has been criticised by some as creating 'temples' to art and giving rise to the cult of the celebrity artist.

→

Various evangelical church movements are growing fast in both the UK and USA. This one occupied by The Potter's House in the former Savoy Cinema in east London, designed by George Coles, represents the church's ability to colonise abandoned pockets of urban space and adapt to societal changes at grass roots levels.

era. Pluralism and the loss of this monopoly over the use of sacred space presents both an opportunity and a challenge for architects.

And what of the future for religious architecture? The contradictions of modernity that bring in to being so-called fundamentalist religious terrorist groups that can exist in non-localized communities thanks to ultra-sophisticated radio and internet technology. Their recruits are often from developed countries, and also spawn hybrid, more benign religious denominations.

Peter Berger, in his book *The Homeless Mind* [13], drew attention to the disruptive effect of increasingly mobile, individualized societies – what Zygmunt Bauman calls 'Liquid Modernity' – in which change is the norm: 'Modern man has suffered from a deepening condition of 'homelessness' ... The correlation of the migratory character of his experience of society and of self has been what might be called a metaphysical loss of 'home'. It goes without saying that this condition is psychologically hard to bear.' [14] The public philosopher Alain de Botton recently called for the construction of a series of 'atheist temples' within which people who do not believe in God could find meaning. De Botton worked with two RCA students, Jordan Hodgson and Tom Greenall, to provide speculative designs for what could be an interesting new typology. In London the phenomenon already has a congregation behind it, if not a building, with Sunday 'atheist church' services regularly pulling in hundreds of (non)believers. [15]

The creep of transcendent spaces into non-religious programmes also poses an exciting challenge for architects: what is the appropriate language to describe, say, shops and art galleries when they ape sacred spaces? And will the fast-growing Protestant evangelical sects, whose congregations are currently disparate and relatively small, start to demand and commission more complex venues than those which suit their current requirements

13
Peter Berger, *The Homeless Mind: Modernization and Conciousness*, Random House, 1973
14
Zygmunt Bauman, *Liquid Modernity*, Polity Press, 2000
15
Alain de Botton, 'There's No Room For Doubt', *Architect's Journal*, February 2012

for large-volume spaces: a good sound system and – in the US at least – large car parks? At the moment these churches can be found in industrial estates around the UK, but with an increase in the number of adherents may come demands for more permanent, ostentatious bases.

The shifting centre of economic and political gravity can reasonably be expected to continue to move eastwards, away from the North Atlantic countries to Asian and South American ones, and the resultant work that will come out of this will be worth watching, especially when, in comparison with Indian and Chinese populations, the Judaeo-Christian world is so small: there are more Chinese citizens in China (1,320 million) than Muslims, of all varieties, worldwide (1,270 million), and only slightly more Catholics in the world than Indians in India (1.270 million versus 1,130 million). [16] The macro- and micro-political shifts that help power this global transition, from falling imports, to widespread redundancies, will continue to fuel the existential angst of late modernity that, for some, is mollified and given meaning by religion. We can be sure that people will keep on believing, and that architects will continue building sacred spaces.

16
Vatican figures on religion from *International Herald Tribune*, 31 March 2009; and population figures from the World Bank

INTRODUCTION

CONGREGATION

CONGREGATION

Before the church comes the people. Many people find that great solace can be found in participating in religious gatherings through the sense of congregation with one's fellow men and women. Though individual contemplation is encouraged by many religions, most give primacy to the collective gathering as part of their means of worship. This is common to many faiths, whether the context is a mosque, synagogue, chapel or temple. In the act of congregation, scale is not so important – be it four or five teenagers lying prostrate on gym mats making their prayers towards Mecca, or Midnight Mass on Christmas Eve attended by hundreds under the soaring vaults of Durham Cathedral – what matters is the gathering of people, for one shared purpose.

Over long periods of time, these shared gatherings grew large enough to demand dedicated spaces of their own. The spatial and programmatic requirements across most faiths do not differ a great deal – in essence, a large room for gathering together is at the crux of most religious buildings. But typically, these spaces, whether large or small, formal or informal, must be able not just to host worship, but also to offer something to the community that goes beyond the spiritual. That may be practical or symbolic or, more often, a combination of the two.

At the Church of Seed chapel, situated in Guangdong province on the mountain of Luofu (page 46), a gift to the community was made in the form of a sensitively articulated gathering space. Considered a sacred landscape and the location of many historic temples, the client was eager that the new church should not be seen as an aggressive impostor in an area of significance to the Taoist and Buddhist faiths, so it needed to tread lightly in its landscape. By making the roof of the church a stepped viewing platform that could be used for walkers and pilgrims of any faith to contemplate the area beyond, the architects provided the community with an inclusive and sympathetic new work of religious architecture.

At the Shrine of the Virgin of La Antigua in the Rioja region of Spain (page 52), Otxotorena Arquitectos were tasked with building a shrine for the villagers of the nearby settlement of Alberite which would incorporate an existing stone archway, a remnant which had been salvaged by villagers from demolition then maintained and preserved ever since. Because the new building incorporates, celebrates and respects the arch, the architects have been able to be attentive to the sensibilities of the congregation, for which, arguably, this built fabric is part of both a built and a religious tradition.

Office for Peripheral Architecture's Kärsämäki Single Church in Finland (page 28), harks back to pre-industrial days and a less sophisticated division of labour within the building trades. Here the brief to use only eighteenth-century building and carpentry methods, and exclusively rely on horse- and man-power to erect the building took the community back to a time when the raising of a barn, or the building of a church, would have been something which involved the whole village: a piece of collective labour that was a joyful and spectacular event in itself. Sharing characteristics with the church in Kärsämäki, Beton's Wooden Church in Poland (page 34), illustrates an instrumentalist approach to the way in which the building of a church can shape the social aspects of a community. On the banks of the Vistula River as it passes through the village of Tarnow in southeast Poland, Beton were tasked with creating a place of worship which would gently steer the behaviour of a congregation it serves, as well as cater to the spiritual needs of its locals and passersby. Located in a popular spot for summer trips and lazy getaways from the city, the chapel's client was concerned that this idyllic landscape was in danger of being spoilt by day-trippers. So here the presence of a spiritual building is partly intended to exert a controlling or moderating influence on the people who may encounter it. The construction of the building was also intended to serve a social purpose: it was designed to be built by local craftsmen, the intention being that in coming together and working on this local project, they would feel very much part of the body and soul of the small woodland chapel.

There are some buildings that can catch a moment, or become well loved over a period of time – by both citizens and visitors alike – to become symbols of a city, intrinsically linked to a place's identity. This has happened in the case of the simple but memorable form of the Cardboard Cathedral in Christchurch, New Zealand by Shigeru Ban (page 22), built as a temporary replacement for the city's Victorian cathedral, which was irrevocably damaged in an earthquake that left 185 people dead. Designed by Ban for no fee, its existence is a reminder of the ways in which buildings can become hubs for people to come together in times of adversity and how the soothing affect of architecture can act as an emollient in difficult times.

Though rich in meaning and architecturally inspiring, most of the buildings which follow in this chapter arc spatially straightforward, giving primacy to their function of gathering people together in human congregation. None lose sight of the most important element that will bring them to life: the people.

Such is the association of cathedrals with solidity that the notion of building one from cardboard seems almost absurd. We think of cathedrals as places of permanence: the places through which generations upon generations will pass, the rocks upon which the church of the people is built. In Britain, the possession of a cathedral has long been synonymous with the notion of a city, a relic of Henry VIII's creation of six dioceses in sixteenth-century England and his granting each of these sees city status. The idea of a less-than-permanent cathedral then is surely a radical proposal. But that is exactly what Shigeru Ban proposed and built in the New Zealand city of Christchurch.

Located in a geologically volatile city, the 131-year-old Christchurch Cathedral was ripped apart in February 2011 by an earthquake measuring 6.3 on the Richter scale. The quake devastated the city, killing 185 people and toppling Christchurch's cathedral spire, and inflicting major structural damage. Subsequent earthquakes in the June and December of the same year ruined its rose window and after extensive surveys it was decided not to restore the cathedral. It was deconsecrated and demolition began, ending the days of the first Christchurch Cathedral, initially designed in the 1860s, from England, by the British architect Sir George Gilbert Scott, who never visited the site.

Shigeru Ban became involved while he was working on the recovery efforts of another disaster – the March 11, 2011 earthquake that hit the coast of Japan, triggering a tsunami and a nuclear accident, just a month after the tragedy in New Zealand. Solidarity between the two countries was strong – forty-eight Japanese nationals had died in the Christchurch earthquake and Japan had sent a search-and-rescue team to comb the city's debris in the aftermath of the tremors. After being contacted by the diocese about plans to construct a temporary venue, Ban agreed, offered to work for free, and plans unfolded for a temporary cathedral, to be built two blocks southeast of the original site.

Ban's approach was radical, but it built upon work he had done over a number of decades in disaster zones, beginning with his work in Vietnam after the 1995 Kobe earthquake and his subsequent efforts in storm-torn India, Taiwan and Haiti. Using unconventional building methods he is able to quickly fashion habitable shelters for the dispossessed, suffering in the wake of natural disasters. The Christchurch building is made from paper, cardboard tubes, timber and steel shipping containers, a tried-and-tested palette which Ban had used in his disaster-relief projects. The cathedral's walls are made from shipping containers, which host ancillary functions, and above these a 21 metre (69 foot) high A-frame made from ninety-eight equally sized cardboard tubes, reinforced with laminated timber beams, creates the nave. The nave tapers slightly towards the altar, creating a trapezoidal plan. Triangular sheets of coloured stained glass nod to the rose window of the 1868 Gilbert Scott cathedral. A polycarbonate roof, coated with waterproof polyurethane and flame-retardants, keeps the rain out, and stops it from impregnating the cardboard.

Unlike concrete, this combination of timber and paper performs well under earthquake conditions and the building is thought to be one of the safest, most earthquake-proof buildings in Christchurch. The cathedral is just one building in Shigeru Ban's back catalogue which helped the Japanese architect win the Pritzker Architecture Prize in 2014. Expected to have a life of approximately fifty years, the new cathedral seats 700 people and has quickly become a well-loved Christchurch icon.

CARDBOARD CATHEDRAL

Shigeru Ban | Christchurch, New Zealand, 2013

1↓ 2→

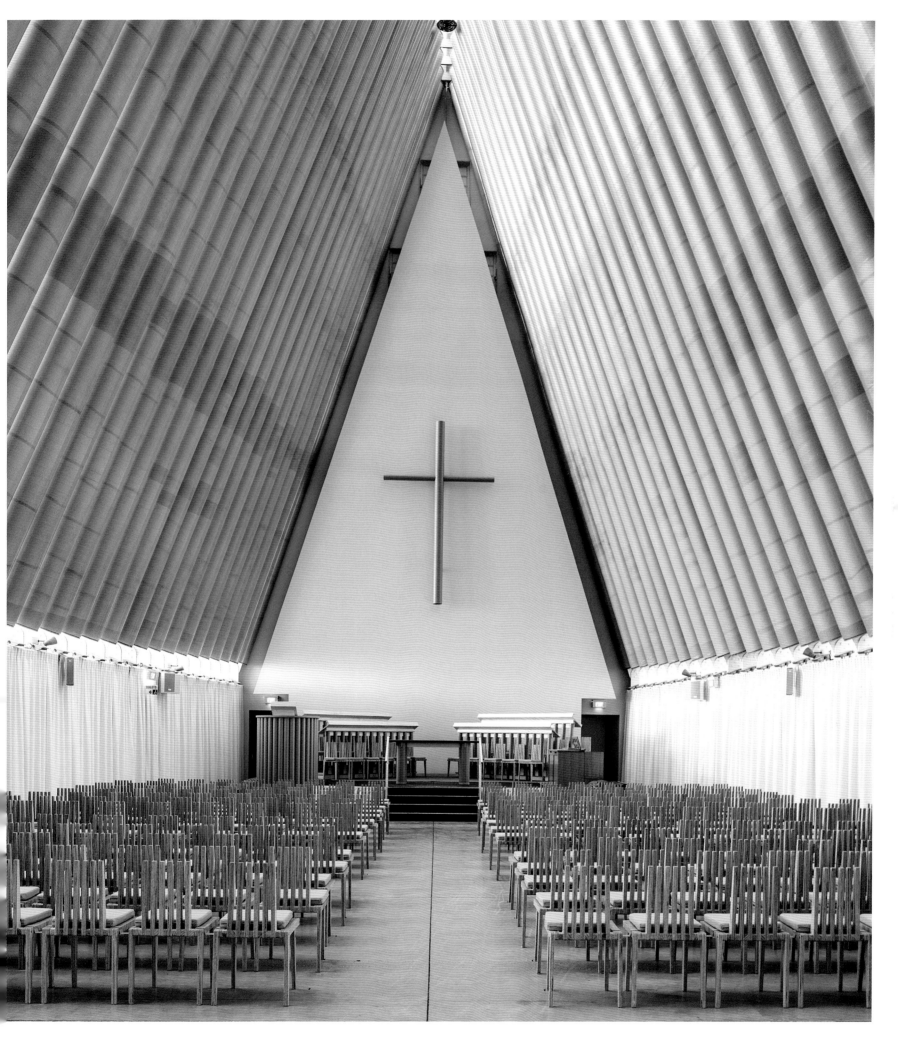

CARDBOARD CATHEDRAL Shigeru Ban

1
The steeply pitched A-frame roof of the cathedral is clad in clear polycarbonate sheeting while shipping containers have been placed on the two long sides to accommodate ancillary functions.

2
A view of the interior looking down the nave towards the altar underneath the steeply pitched cardboard tube-lined ceiling.

3
Floor plan: The cathedral tapers from the entrance to the nave, drawing worshippers into the space.

4
Detail view of the stained glass windows which, along with strips of the clear polycarbonate roof sheeting, bring natural light into the cathedral and reference the rose window of the earlier Gilbert Scott cathedral.

5
Section: The cathedral's structural A-frame is formed of ninety-eight cardboard tubes reinforced with laminated timber beams, which stand twenty-one metres high and form the nave.

6
The view from the altar looking back towards the entrance. Simple white curtains screen access to the shipping containers adjacent.

7
The entrance to the cathedral is through a modified shipping container, over which a large section of the carboard tube structure creates a deep porch, set with triangles of stained glass.

↑ 3   ↓ 4   5 →

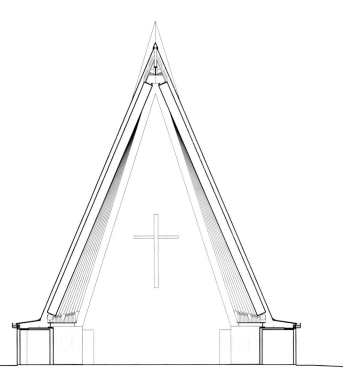

6 ↑ 7 ↓

CARDBOARD CATHEDRAL Shigeru Ban

8
Within the cathedral, private spaces are screened by curved walls made of the same carboard tubes that line the ceiling.

9
The side chapels, accommodated in shipping containers, are screened from the main space by fins of cardboard tubing.

10
Exploded axonometric: The simplicity of the architectural elements is illustrated here, including the polycarbonate roofing, carboard tubes, shipping containers and the triangular end walls.

11
The lectern employs the same cardboard tubing as used elsewhere in the cathedral.

8↑   9↓

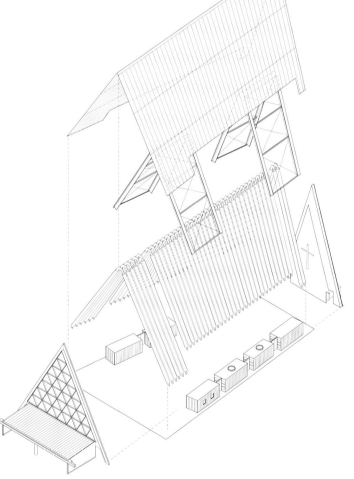

←10 11↑

CARDBOARD CATHEDRAL   **Shigeru Ban**

For all its formal sobriety, the Kärsämäki Shingle Church hums with an eerie, otherworldly presence. Situated on a bend in the Pyhäjoki River, surrounded by fields, the church was built on the same site that parishioners of Kärsämäki, in the north of Finland, had first built a church over a quarter of a millenia ago in 1765. Eventually the congregation outgrew the church and after falling into disrepair the original church was demolished in 1841. No plans or drawings remained to indicate what the original parish church looked like. Hence the conceit, when an international design competition was announced, that the new building should honour its predecessor by using eighteenth-century building techniques for the construction of a modern church. Lassila Hirvilammi Architects (now Office for Peripheral Architecture) responded with a building that marries rustic techniques with a contemporary taste for stripped-down, pared-back forms.

Square in plan, with squat, shingle-clad elevations beneath pitched roofs, there is a typological purity to the church that evokes a child's drawing of a house. The lantern at the building's peak nods to traditional bell towers. The corners of the windowless facades have openings to the core of the building. At the front are large apertures in the shingle exterior that shore the timber core within, and on the other corners of the square are large lightdoors, made from agricultural-style folding doors. The architects refer to this arrangement between the internal, load-bearing structure and the external shingled skin as 'the core and the cloak'. The shingle envelope hangs from the load-bearing structure, ending a short distance from the ground. The resulting effect is of the building hovering, which further amplifies its uncanny character. The functional spaces of the church – vestry, vestibules and store rooms – are housed in the space between the 'core' and the 'cloak'. This liminal space also prepares the visitor for the unique atmosphere of the church, passing as they do from the daylight into a dimly lit corridor, and then back into the bright centre of the church, which is lit from above by natural light. At night the church is illuminated by the moon and moveable, candle-lit glass and tinplate lanterns carried by the congregation.

In keeping with the peculiar requirements of the brief, the timber for the load-bearing log frame was felled from forests owned by the parish and partly transported by horse-power. The logs were either hand-sawn or cut at the old sawmill nearby. The frame's notched corner joints were created with traditional hand tools including axes, saws and chisels. The use of these old construction methods required considerable research into the most appropriate tools and techniques, and in some instances the design and making of new implements.

Sweat and muscle erected the church: a third of the log frame was built by hand in a nearby field and when the foundations had been prepared, the entire structure was moved into position. The shingles that give the church its name were made of aspen and were then hand-whittled – all fifty thousand of them. Prior to being affixed to the frame, the shingles were dipped in hot tar, giving them their blackened appearance and their important weatherproofing capabilities. Such apparently simple techniques proved to require a sophisticated design and craft sensibility. The result is a richly detailed, yet modest building. Viewed from afar, the church is a quiet, self-confident presence in the bucolic landscape. Within, all is calm.

KÄRSÄMÄKI SHINGLE CHURCH
Office for Peripheral Architecture | Kärsämäki, Finland, 2004

1↓

1
The church bell tower stands as a separate beacon to the main building, straddling the wooden boardwalk that leads across the lawn to the church entrance.

2
The new, modern church that replaces the historic structure comprises two base elements – a log-built structural 'core' that is wrapped by a black, tarred and shingle-clad 'cloak'.

3
Situated beside the Pyhäjoki River, the first church in the parish of Kärsämäki was completed in 1765 but after two centuries of use, the building became too small for the congregation. As it was already dilapidated, it was eventually demolished in 1841.

2↑ 3↓

KÄRSÄMÄKI SHINGLE CHURCH **Office for Peripheral Architecture**

4↑ 5↓

4
Though the exact site of the original church was documented, its appearance remained unknown – hence the conceit to build a modern church with eighteenth-century building techniques.

5
Each of the fifty thousand shingles needed for the roofing and cladding is made of split aspen, which was then finished by whittling. Finally, they were dipped in hot tar prior to being fixed in place.

6
Corners to the windowless building are pierced by openings to the core. The large northeastern apertures admit light while other corners are large light-doors that reference an agricultural style.

7
Floor plan: The building is entered either via a short flight of steps or by two shallow ramps that meet in the northeast corner in a square entrance vestibule.

8
Section: The timber for the load-bearing log frame were felled from forests owned by the parish. The logs were either hand-sawn or cut at the old sawmill, and brought to the site by horse-power.

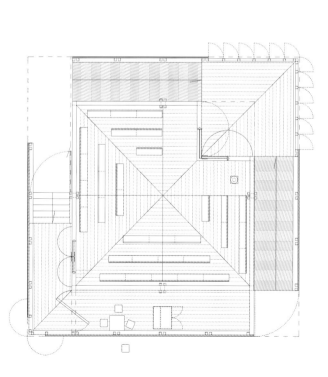

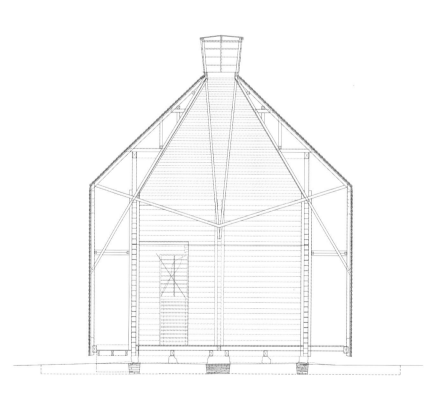

KÄRSÄMÄKI SHINGLE CHURCH   **Office for Peripheral Architecture**

The shingle envelope hangs from the load-bearing structure and finishes just above the ground. In effect, the tarred skin appears to hover, which amplifies the uncanny character of the building.

10
The notched corner joints were created with traditional hand tools, including axes, saws and chisels. To emulate these methods, several implements had to be designed and made anew.

11
There is no fixed seating in the church and the altar is movable, enabling the church to be set up for a variety of functions and uses.

12
Natural light enters the interior from a rooflight; during the darker hours it is complemented by candle-lit glass and tinplate lanterns, held by the congregation.

9↑ 10↓   11↓ 12→

KÄRSÄMÄKI SHINGLE CHURCH **Office for Peripheral Architecture**

Set in a woodland glade beside a river, there's something about this chapel that conjures up images from the Grimm brothers' fairy tales. From afar, its silhouette resembles a bishop's mitre, a witch's hat, or a hunter's cap. Though completed in 2009, by a young metropolitan practice, there's something atavistic and slightly uncanny about this elemental timber chapel.

It is the work of the young Polish studio Beton, the practice of husband-and-wife team Marta Rowińska and Lech Rowiński. The two met at architecture school, Marta having previously studied fashion design. The name of their practice, Beton, which suggests associations with concrete, belies a flexibility of method, their multi-disciplinary approach seeing their work encompass graphics, clothing and buildings. In the past the pair have created wearable folding fabric constructions and worked in industrial design, but for this project the two adapted simple timber construction methods.

The chapel is situated on the tree-lined banks of the Vistula River in southeast Poland, a popular spot for summer sun-seekers and day-trippers. The brief was two-fold – not just to create a small chapel on the outskirts of Tarnów, but for the building to be constructed by members of the local community in the hope of uniting them through shared toil on the project.

The project was only made more unusual since the client was not one of the local Roman Catholic dioceses, but rather an anonymous Polish writer. This author was keen to preserve the surrounding natural beauty, something they felt was under threat from tourists and pleasure seekers, and the temporary structures and rubbish they were leaving in their wake. It was hoped that the presence of a church nearby – and the respect that this type of building commands in the local region – would temper the behaviour of the holiday-makers and prevent the precious location from becoming a litter-strewn tourist trap.

Beton's response to these demands was to create an elegant yet simple structure which could be constructed using straightforward carpentry techniques, seeing as the local community with limited specialist skills was to take charge of construction. A barn-like building, set on a concrete foundation, was therefore ideal.

The chapel has a simple, windowless front elevation, clad in spruce, which tapers to a triangular spire. On to this an undecorated cross is fixed. The flanks of the church are similarly window free and are covered with feathery aspen shingles, fixed in a herringbone pattern. These hang from a structure made from twelve composite wall and roof trusses made from honey-coloured local spruce set at 1.2 metre (4 foot) intervals, laterally braced by diagonal members along the wall plane. The interior sequencing is also straightforward: an eight-bay nave – without a sacristy or other ancillary spaces – is preceded by a three-bay ante-room. Visitors to the chapel sit on wooden benches. An understated crucifix behind the altar is the sole overtly Roman Catholic decoration, and the lack of adornment and the austere construction makes for a contemplative space. The visitor's focus is then automatically drawn to the prominent window behind the altar – the only glazing in the chapel – where the whole south wall is glazed; rather than through any overtly religious iconography, the divine is invoked by the changing beauty and power of nature. Detailing is simple, creating an unfussy vernacular architecture that achieves its power from a neat synthesis between materials, their proportions, and the way the chapel sits within its landscape.

WOODEN CHURCH

Beton | Tarnów, Poland, 2009

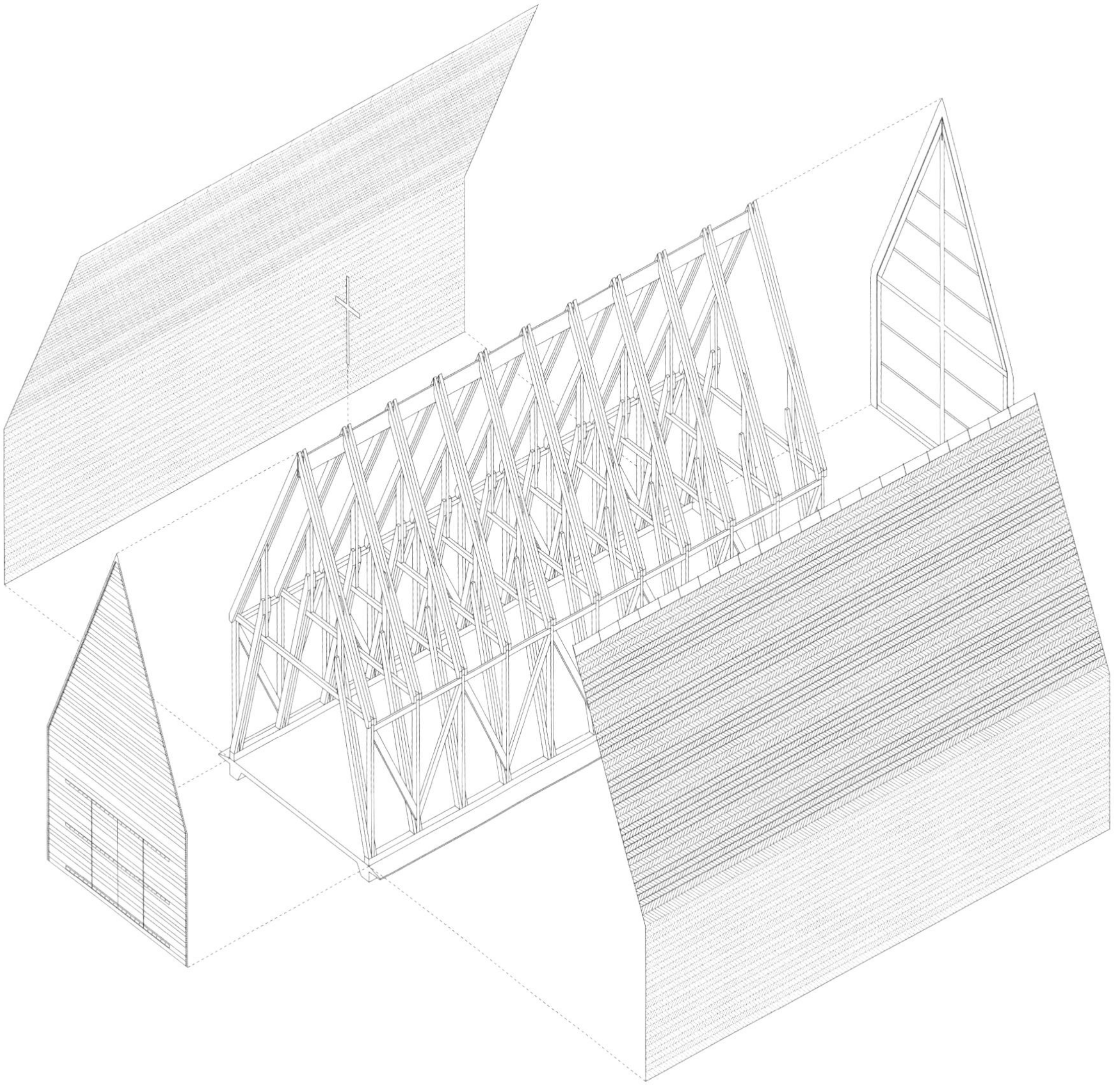

↑1 2→

WOODEN CHURCH **Beton**

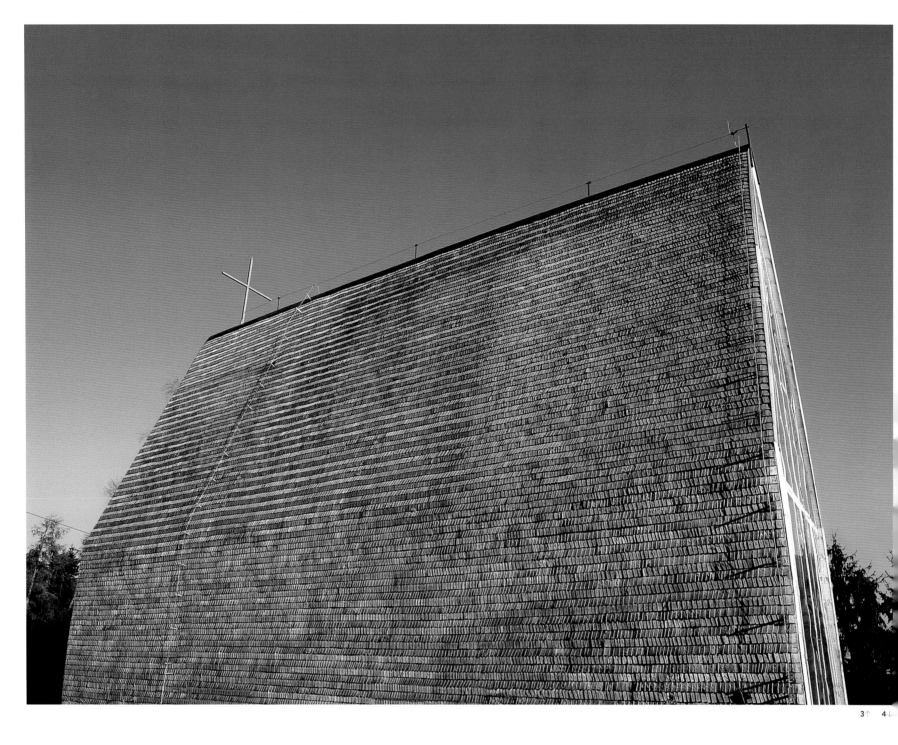

3↑   4↓

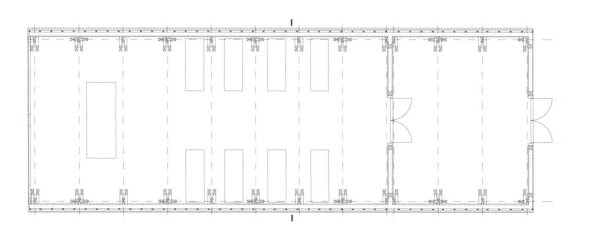

CONGREGATION   36

1
Exploded axonometric: The construction is simply composed of twelve composite wall and roof trusses set at 1.2 metre (4 foot) intervals that support the shingled building envelope.

2
Commissioned by an independent client, the church was seen as a means to protect the integrity of the site, near a popular scenic location on the Vistula River.

3
Formed of thousands of small aspen shingles, the sloping wooden roof seamlessly falls to become upright church walls.

4
Floor plan: The simple rectangular space is organised into a three-bay ante-room followed by an eight-bay nave in which visitors sit on simple wooden benches.

5
Section: A single unadorned cross affixed to the apex is the only external religious reference of the church. The building provides a place for worship as well as for contemplation of the surrounding natural environment.

6
Arranged in a herringbone pattern, the aspen shingles are affixed to a cross-braced spruce frame, the timber for which was harvested from trees nearby.

7
Section: To encourage the participation of local community members with little building experience, the wooden structure is deliberately designed to be simple.

↙5 6↑ 7↓

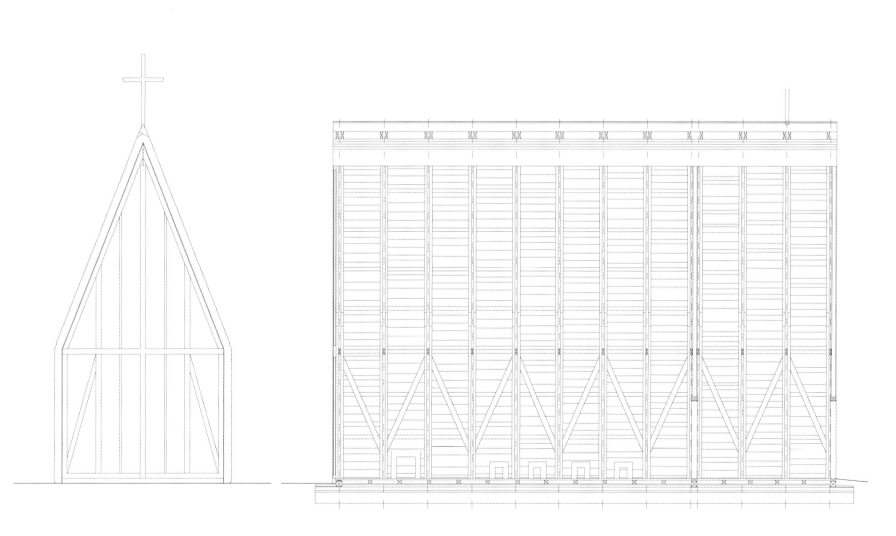

8

Honey-coloured spruce trusses rise 10 metres (33 feet) high and are complemented by a spruce lining that creates a sense of warmth within the chapel.

9

Composed almost entirely of timber, the large glazed wall behind the altar is an exception, admitting natural light into the interior. A simple concrete slab forms the building's floor and foundations.

←8

At the foothills of the Andes Mountains, just 50 kilometres (31 miles) from the Peruvian capital of Lima, is the district of Cieneguilla. Sitting within the valley created by the Lurín River which originates in the glaciers and lagoons of the western Andes, it's one of the few areas in the vicinity not to be taken over by Lima's suburban sprawl. In this relatively verdant environment is the De la Piedra Chapel, designed by Peruvian practice Nómena Arquitectos. The building's impressive cloister has created a pathway that serves spiritual and practical functions, both enclosing the chapel and leading the visitor to it.

The chapel, a private commission, is located in the grounds of the client's house, a short walk away from the main residence. When planning the layout and procession from house to chapel, the architects looked to Le Corbusier's study of proportions found in nature, in particular the Fibonacci sequence of numbers found within the spiral of a seashell and his 'Modulor' system of measurements, based upon the dimensions of the human body. These proportions were used as the basis for the height of the walls, as well as the windows, doors and ceilings throughout. In plan, the chapel follows a kind of orthogonal spiral, with the space

of worship at the centre, held like a precious object cradled within the crook of an arm. A long wall and a raised pool of water at knee height define the long approach to the chapel from the open garden setting.

The mass of the building is set in concrete and the suggestion of the horizontally banded timber formwork provides a datum that unites the chapel and the approach wall. For the architects, this articulates the transition from the open space, given to profane activities, and to the interior enclosed space, devoted to the sacred. At the end of this processional route is an enclosed patio space with a seating area, a liminal space where visitors can gather between the exposed area outside and the intimate area within the body of the chapel. A large single door, matching the offset square proportions generated by the Fibonacci sequence, spins on a hinge, allowing the visitor into the chapel, the nucleus of the building. Once inside, the feeling of compression set up by the low enclosures of pathway and patio is released by stepping into a triple-height space. This play of compression and release echoes moments in Frank Lloyd Wright's architecture, and in particular one of Álvaro Siza Vieira's early works, the Boa Nova Tea House in

Porto, Portugal where an architectural promenade, lined by painted concrete walls, presents dramatic perspectives of the landscape as it alternatively hides and reveals the sea and the horizon line.

Inside, the chapel has an offset grid of small oriel windows that allow light to puncture the space and which naturally ventilate the tower. They also allow glimpses of the surrounding countryside from within during the day, and the converse at night. The cold concrete is tempered by simple timber pews in the austere room – the only decoration comes from the uplighters and the shuttering marks of the poured concrete.

Despite the apparent strict delineation between sacred and profane, the chapel can be used in different ways; while the chapel is able to remain a quiet space for contemplation, for big occasions, large congregations can gather outside. The doors behind the altar slide open to offer views out on to the lawn, where a crowd can congregate, enclosed by the processional walkway to the chapel. Seen from the other side of its walls, the triple-height worship space forms a beacon, the wall both a protective line and a conduit, bringing people into the chapel.

DE LA PIEDRA CHAPEL
Nómena Arquitectos + Ximena Alvarez | Cieneguilla, Peru, 2010

1↓   2→

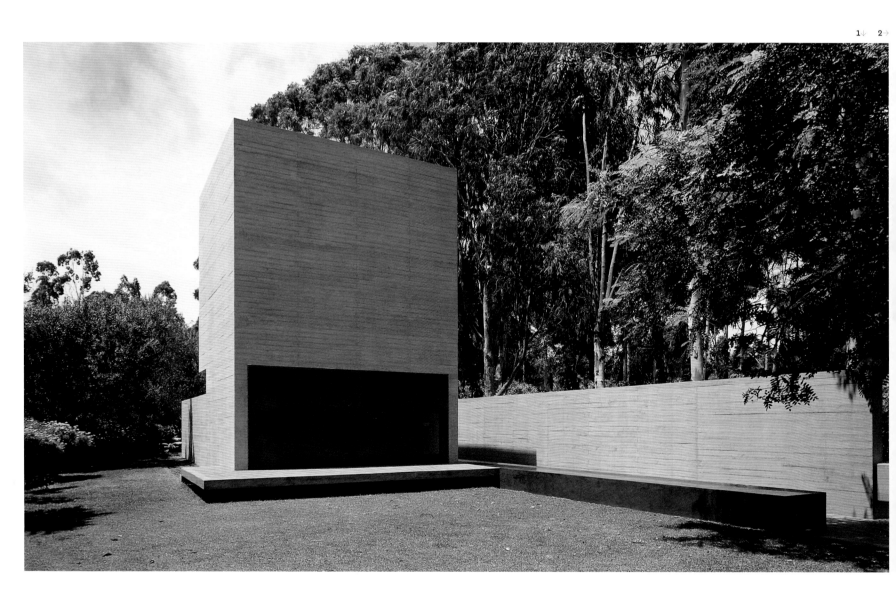

DE LA PIEDRA CHAPEL Nómena Arquitectos + Ximena Alvarez

1

Located in the grounds of the client's house, the entry procession and chapel itself are carefully planned in accord with natural proportions studied by Le Corbusier, such as the Fibonacci sequence.

2

The processional route to the small orthogonal chapel from the open gardens is defined by a linear path that passes a raised pool of water and reaches an enclosed patio where visitors can gather.

3

From afar, the triple-height worship space forms a beacon; its walls are both protective as well as acting as a conduit to draw people into the chapel.

4

Floor plan: The chapel forms an orthogonal spiral, with the space of worship at the centre, cradled within a series of protective walls.

5

The horizontally banded concrete is marked by its timber formwork and provides a datum that unites the church and the approach wall while marking the transition from profane to sacred.

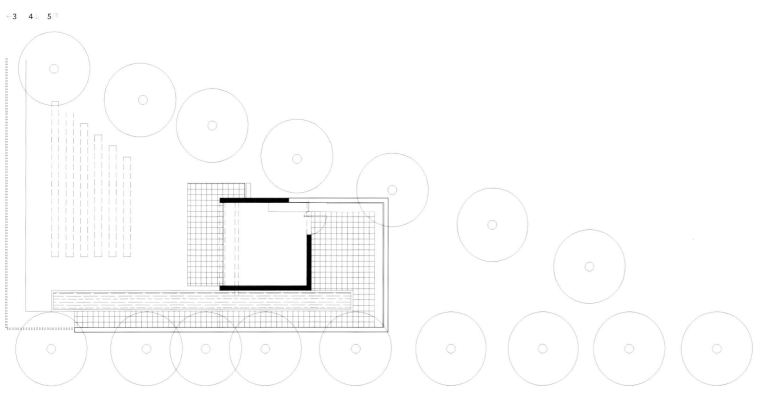

←3   4↓   5↱

6
A large single pivoting door, with offset square proportions that echo the Fibonacci sequence, allow entry into the body of the chapel.

7
The austere interior is tempered by simple timber pews, spare up-lighting, and the marks of shuttering carried by the poured concrete walls.

8
Cross section: Le Corbusier's 'Le Modulor' proportions are clearly marked on the exterior of the entry door.

9
An off-set grid of small oriel windows allow light to puncture the space and naturally ventilate the tower. They allow glimpses of the countryside by day and indicate occupancy by night.

10
Long section: The feeling of compression set up by the enclosed low pathway and patio contrasts with the expansive feel of the triple-height chapel space.

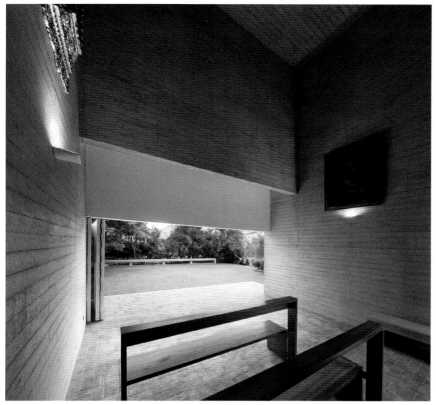

← 6 7↑ 8↓

9↑ 10↓

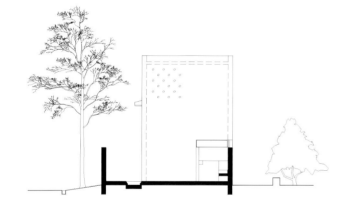

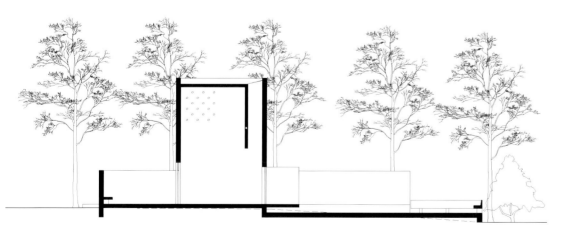

DE LA PIEDRA CHAPEL   **Nómena Arquitectos + Ximena Alvarez**

On the north bank of the Dong River, in China's Guangdong province, is Mount Luofu, one of the country's seven most sacred mountains. Of special spiritual significance to Buddhists and Taoists, the mountain is where, during the Eastern Jin dynasty, the legendary alchemist Ge Hong was said to have refined his elixirs and where the 'Well of Longevity', the place from which he drew his water, is to be found.

There are many historic temples on the mountain due to its religious significance: the Temple of Emptiness, the Temple of Junkets, the Temple of the Nine Heavens, the Temple of the White Crane, the Temple of the Yellow Dragon and the Wa Sau Toi temple which is linked to both the Dragon and Bak Mei styles of Kung Fu. Until recently, however, there have been very few Christian places of worship. The first was the Church of Seed, built by the Hong Kong practice O Studio Architects in 2011 for a client who had built private houses in the area, with the Guangzhou Architectural Engineering Design Institute acting as project architects. In this context its name may suggest a desire to proselytize, that the church may become a spot from where new converts to Christianity may spring. However, the intention was that as well as offering a place for local Chris-

tians to worship, the church would serve as a recreation and gathering space for villagers from the nearby area. Given its aims, overtly religious symbolism is kept to a minimum and the moveable seating creates a flexible space which can be converted from service-room to a more humdrum, though appreciated, function area.

Viewed from afar, the church appears as a cylindrical form punctuated by a diagonal slash through its stepped roofline. In reality, it's more like three separate curved walls, joined by doorways, which wrap around the church's interior gathering space. These walls give the church its name, the walls curling around the building's interior reminiscent of the casing around the seed of a plant. The architects have made a gift to the local community in the form of the accessible rooftop terrace, a place that allows visitors to contemplate the beauty of the mountain – something that seekers of spiritual solace have been doing for thousands of years – from an elevated vantage point.

Inside, this stepped roof terrace has the effect of introducing a dramatic change in ceiling levels – its three-metre height at the church's entrance rises to twelve metres behind the altar. The sanctuary space and altar are

very plain, accented only by two raised concrete steps – a simple language of thresholds that throughout the building mark the transition to a more sacred space. Offset to the left of the altar on the southeast-facing wall is a cruciform opening that not only allows morning sun into the interior of the church, but also provides a visible beacon of the cross that can be seen from across the valley. The west wall is windowless and blocks the strong afternoon sun while the north-facing wall hides the toilet blocks.

The material language is simple and raw, making the most of local, easily worked materials like bamboo and using a vocabulary that fits well in its environment. The main structure was constructed from in situ concrete made with bamboo formwork. The regular vertical lines of the bamboo formwork give a kind of rustication and striation to the building, which helps break up its mass, and help it to fit into the surroundings. The chairs and tables used within the church are also made from bamboo, echoing the materials familiar to village life, and their simplicity gives a ceremony and power to the mass and light within the church.

CHURCH OF SEED
O Studio Architects | Mount Luofu, China, 2011

1↓ 2→

CHURCH OF SEED

O Studio Architects

The Church of Seed appears cylindrical from afar and is one of many historical places of worship on Mount Luofu, which is among China's most sacred mountains.

2

The material language of the church is simple and raw: the majority of the structure is made from in situ concrete held by bamboo formwork.

3

A cruciform incision into the southeast wall, offset from the altar, provides a visible beacon of the church and admits morning sun into the interior.

4

The roof terrace is accessible to the public and allows the local community an elevated place from which to contemplate the beauty of the mountain.

5

Visitors approach to the entry reveals the raking tiered glass ceiling of the interior worship space, which is wrapped by robust concrete walls.

6

Section: The interior worship space responds to the stepped roof terrace, rising from 3 metres at the entrance to an apex of 12 metres above the altar.

7

Floor plan: A series of three separate curved walls, joined by doorways, wrap around the central worship space. Reminiscent of a plant's seed casing, the walls give the church its name.

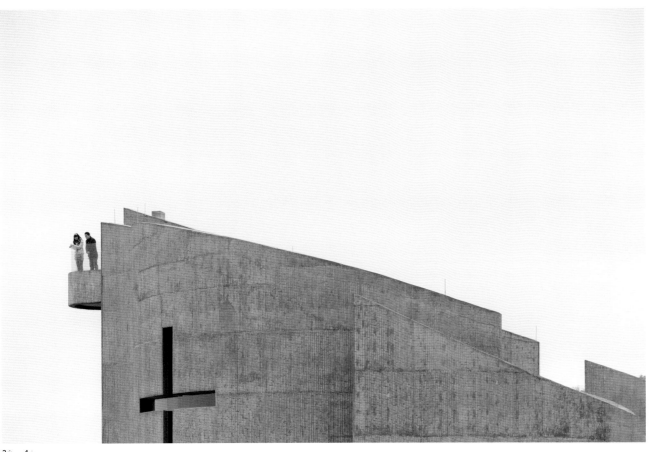

3↑ 4↓

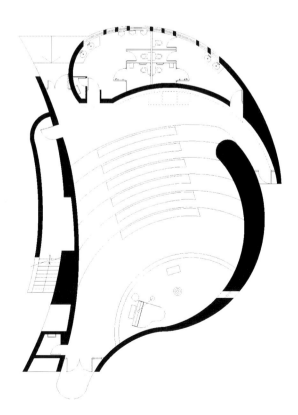

CHURCH OF SEED **O Studio Architects**

8
Within the central gathering space, overt religious symbolism is kept to a minimum: the altar is modestly marked by two steps and all furniture can be moved easily to accommodate other uses of the room.

9
Tables and chairs are made from the readily available and familiar material of bamboo. Similarly, walls are clad in bamboo lengths and the concrete formwork carries the texture of its bamboo shuttering.

10
The stepped concrete ceiling resembles folds of fabric and admits clerestory light; the asymmetric incised cross-shaped window behind the altar is the only obvious religious motif in the room.

8↑ 9↓ 10→

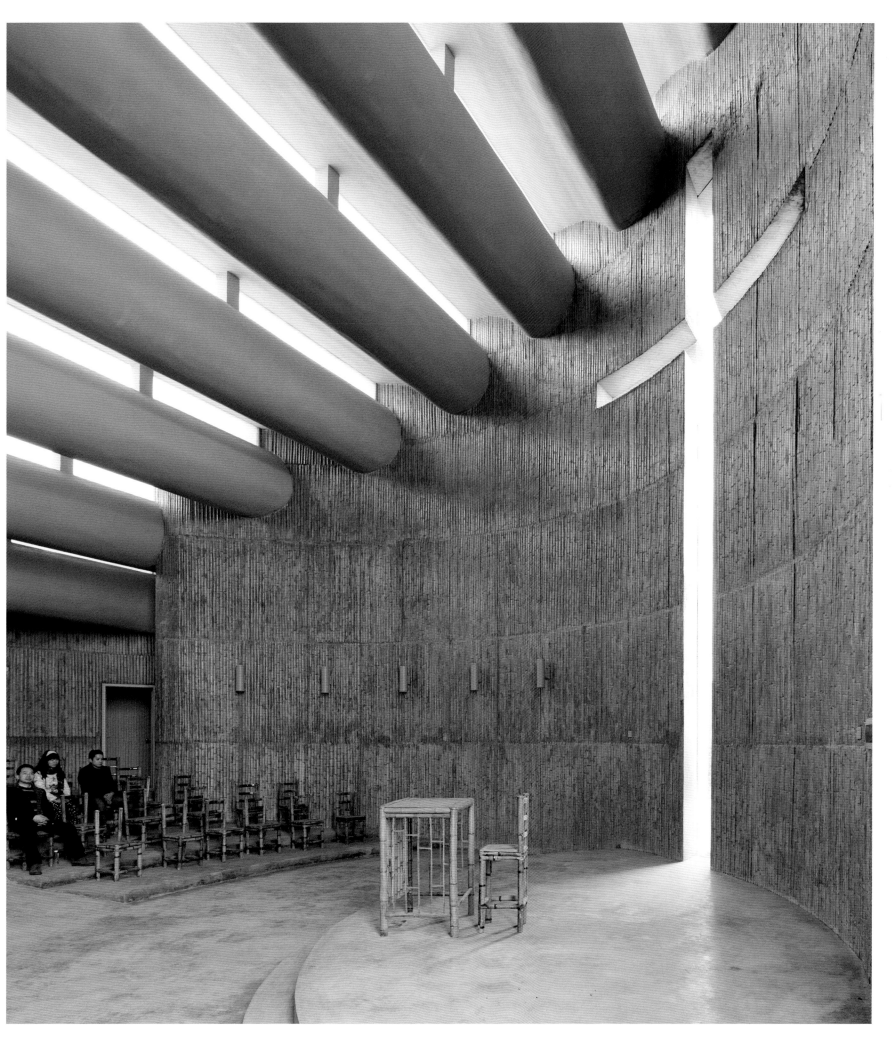

51   **CHURCH OF SEED**   **O Studio Architects**

Its pilotis, sun-bleached concrete and asymmetric elevations bring to mind the classic Brazilian mid-century Modernism of Oscar Niemeyer, yet this elegant little hillside chapel was built in 2009 by the Pamplona-based architect Juan M. Otxotorena. It is a chapel dedicated to the Virgin Mary, the mother of Christ, sometimes referred to as la Virgen de la Antigua in Spanish. For centuries the Virgin Mary has been a popular devotional figure within the Christian, and more specifically Roman Catholic, faith, especially in Latin countries.

Located in the hills of La Rioja, in the north of Spain, the chapel serves the people of Alberite, a town of approximately 2,500 inhabitants, south of nearby Logroño, an important stop on the Camino de Santiago. This pilgrimage route, terminating in Santiago de Compostela, was popular in medieval times and has recently enjoyed a resurgence among modern-day pilgrims, who take to foot or bicycle to complete it, staying in modest hostels along the way. The site for the shrine was a gift to the parish by the town council. The building was intended to be able to accommodate both private, devotional use by individuals or very small groups as well as large influxes of pilgrims.

It also had to cater for visitors who would come to worship and celebrate on the many Roman Catholic feast days that punctuate the liturgical calendar.

It's a long, low building on top of the plateau of a hillside that overlooks a ravine, and the parish which commissioned it. The chapel is fundamentally a series of outdoor rooms, with the visitor approaching it via a concrete pathway, entering under a piloti over which a flat concrete roof extends above the edge of the path beneath. Once under the canopy, the visitor encounters a remnant of a previous building: a preserved series of stone arches that runs parallel with the new concrete elevation, which greets the visitor as they approach the building. This archway structure was rescued by the villagers of Alberite from a building that was being demolished, and the brief stipulated that the new chapel should incorporate the ruins of the old. The long archway in part dictated the dimensions of the chapel and the concrete walls and roof – which share similarities in colour and texture to the stone of the archways – was conceived as a protective wrap around the building. Meanwhile, the anteroom, reached before the chapel proper, helps to shelter visitors from the rain

and the sun and to frame the views of the surrounding mountains, from which visitors can take spiritual – or just geographical – solace.

Visitors walk from the ante room beneath the canopy along a colonnade created by the archway and the new concrete addition. This takes the visitor to a small chapel with four simple pews. Once inside the chapel, the space opens up somewhat, an extra volume placed along the path-side elevation of the building giving the chapel a much more generous floor-to-ceiling height than the colonnade which leads to it. This play between compression and release helps establish a feeling of peace and space within the chapel. Vertical concrete fins, articulated on the exterior path-facing facade, bring light into the chapel, casting rays of sunlight on to the concrete walls and floor.

Exterior decoration is sparse: a simple concrete cross standing proud of the roof and a single church bell are the only hints of the structure's ecclesiastical nature. Using only one building material, and keeping the shrine low to the ground, helps it to sit easily within its surroundings, and to work with, rather than dominate, the natural beauty of the environment in which it stands.

SHRINE OF THE VIRGIN OF LA ANTIGUA
Otxotorena Arquitectos | Alberite, La Rioja, Spain, 2009

1↓   2→

1

This chapel is located in the hills of La Rioja and serves the local population of Alberite, which neighbours an important pilgrimage site of the Camino de Santiago.

2

Vertical concrete fins, articulated on the exterior path-facing facade, bring light into the chapel and cast rays of sunshine on the concrete walls and floors.

3↑ 4↓

7→

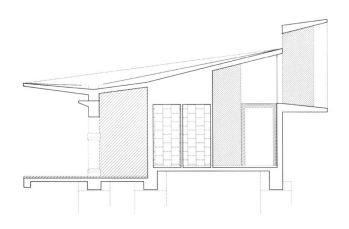

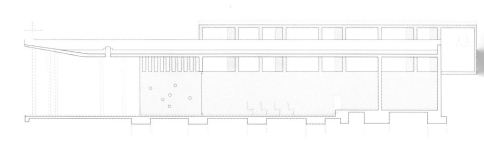

5↑ 6↓

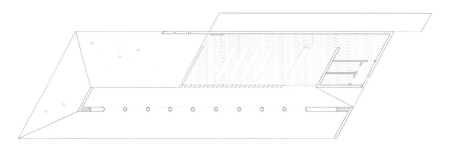

3
The shelter brings together new colonnades and concrete fins with an existing arched stone wall, which was rescued by the villagers of Alberite.

4
Cross section: The transition in height leads visitors from the compressed space of the existing colonnade, to the main chapel, its expanse highlighted by clerestory light that enters through the colonnade of concrete fins.

5
Long section: The shrine is arranged to accommodate a range of uses, including large influxes of pilgrims, small groups, private individual devotion, and celebrations of Roman Catholic feast days.

6
Floor plan: Protected by the concrete canopy, visitors pass from the ante room into a small chapel with four simple pews.

7
The long colonnade of the concrete shelter shares a similar colour palette as the original stone walls and roof, and is conceived of as a protective layer that wraps the building.

55   **SHRINE OF THE VIRGIN OF LA ANTIGUA**   Otxotorena Arquitectos

8↑ 9↓ 10→

8
The ante room, reached before the chapel proper, provides shelter to visitors from the elements and frames views of surrounding mountains.

9
A simple concrete cross that stands proud of the roof and the bells housed in the finned wall are the only external hints of the structure's ecclesiastic nature.

10
The selective use of one building material, and a building that sits close to the ground, allows the shrine to integrate with its surroundings and the existing arched structure.

SHRINE OF THE VIRGIN OF LA ANTIGUA Otxotorena Arquitectos

CLARITY

CLARITY

One of the powerful aspects of the legacy of Modernism is the way in which its core principles have proved so adaptable to different people from across the globe. Just as the spread of Christianity saw evangelists incorporating the rituals of earlier, pagan practices into a Christian context, Modernism has proved a malleable beast, each nation adopting it making its own variants and hybrids.

Alexander Tzonis and Liane Lefaivre indentified this in their essay 'The Grid and the Pathway', and argued that this nuanced adaptation of local custom, what they called critical regionalism, should be encouraged as a means of bringing meaning to an increasingly internationalized design world. Today, the process of renewal, cross-pollination and the spread of ideas has been accelerated by the increasing number of pathways and the greater consumption of media enabled by the explosion in internet use, and the proliferation of image-led architecture and design blogs. A movement can originate in a remote Swiss canton, be broadcast around the world, and then be mimicked in far-flung places, and in turn this work broadcast, continuing the feedback loop. One of the clear movements that has origins in Japan is Minimalism, a useful tag to describe architecture that has been stripped of unnecessary detail. An updated version of Adolf Loos's architecture, famous for its aversion to ornament, and ornamentation's supposedly 'criminal' ways, Minimalism in the early twenty-first century is often more austere than Loos's more sensuous marble-veined creations. Japanese Minimalism has a cultural and spiritual rooting in Japanese Zen philosophy, with its values placed upon simplicity and focusing on essentials. The Japanese rituals of Zen-based Buddhism, the country's dominant belief system, found effective expression in Minimalism, channeling the Japanese aesthetic of 'wabi-sabi': the value of simple and plain objects.

Minimalism, in the time period which this book covers, has been a very attractive language to architects working on the design of sacred spaces. Several of the buildings in this chapter are situated in Asian countries including Japan, China and South Korea and one of the European projects, a centre for retreat and meditation, is a Buddhist centre. The Buddhist Meditation Centre Metta Vihara by Bureau SLA (page 86) follows a simple programme: a set of rooms and a plain hall for meditation, whose detailing and materials are measured and sober throughout. Purity has long been a concern of many religions, metaphorically and literally, whether that be physical cleanliness in Islam, cleanliness of food and its origins in the Jewish faith or purity of the mind and soul in Christianity. An austere architectural language can be a means of articulating this, particularly in an age where, for certain parts of society less, not more, glitz and decoration can signify wealth.

For Toyo Ito, the intention of his Meiso no Mori Municipal Funeral Hall (page 62) was the creation of a secular space within a place of natural beauty that would be an appropriate environment to say one's final goodbyes to loved ones. Here the building was to sit within its beautiful surroundings and not compete with them. With clarity of intent and expression, the building is reduced to one simple star element: the roof. An undulating shell of concrete, it evokes the gentle wafting of a cloud – or a giant lily pad – above the lake and the surrounding 'forest of meditation', after which the crematorium is named. In common with much building work that achieves an effortless poise, there are complex calculations underlying it, in this case parametric geometric formulas which helped define the optimal structure to support its sinuous curves.

At the Church of Water and Light (page 92), the approach was also to work sensitively within the natural environment; in this case the rolling hills and changing skies of the South Korean island of Jeju. The Church's distinctive triangular patterning helps it stand up to, but not rival, the beauty of nature. To complete this effect of being in harmony with nature, the designers placed the church within a moat of water, over which visitors cross to reach the church. Its mix of contemporary construction techniques, minimalist detailing and adaptation of traditional forms is a good example of Tzonis and Liane Lefaivre's critical regionalism. The White Chapel by Jun Aoki & Associates (page 80) represents another example of 'island' typology, the trapezoid-shaped chapel located within the grounds of a hotel. The chapel appears to float on a lake, and is accessed by a small footbridge. A glass wall shielded by circular steel rings doubles as structural supports.

At the St Moritz Church, in the Bavarian city of Augsburg, Germany (page 74), John Pawson has transformed the building's interior, taking away all that was non-essential and reworking the interior lighting to create an intense yet sparse space. The focus was on subtraction and clarification, retaining much of the structure but reducing ornamentation and radically manipulating how light is used throughout. This intensity of approach has proved an attractive means of creating contemporary religious spaces, both for the parishioners of St Moritz, and also the community of Cistercian monks in the Czech Republic, for whom he built new living quarters. One of the criticisms of Minimalism is paradoxically also one of its attractions – its versatility. The same architectural vocabulary can be used to create a retail space, a beauty spa or a place for monks to worship. This can be a dilemma for many designers who find themselves designing religious buildings. That said, the appeal of building sacred spaces with an architecture that emphasizes clarity, quietitude and contemplation in a hectic world, is clear.

Nestled between the base of a wooded hillside, parklands and a large lake in the mountainous Gifu area of Japan, is the cemetery of Kakamigahara, built by the municipality for its 150,000 inhabitants as a special place to mark the end of life. The old crematorium was scheduled to be demolished, so Toyo Ito was free to build a crematorium that was unconstrained by religious content. The building melts into the landscape and provides a simultaneously spiritual and secular setting to commemorate the passing of loved ones. Ito's brief was to create a sublime space that would complement the beauty of its natural setting. The architect was adamant that they would not follow the older structure's attempt – nor indeed that of other crematoria – to reflect the significance of the building's function with a heavily massed building. For the Meiso no Mori funeral hall, which takes its name from the 'forest of meditation' in which it sits, death would not be grim, final and static. Rather, it would be ethereal, part of a continual dance of movements, linked to and part of the air, the trees, the water and the wider natural world.

The result is a delicate and measured building in which the sinuous forms of its incredibly elegant white concrete roof evoke the gentle wafting of a cloud – or a giant lily pad – above the lake. This is a building which deals with the impermanence of life in a grown-up and peaceful way, one that moves with, rather than resists, the ebb and flow of life and death. Behind the effortless lines of the exterior lies some difficult mathematics. Ito worked closely with the structural engineer Mutsuro Sasaki, an expert in parametric design, to create the optimum structure that would support and articulate the thinly profiled roof. Advanced computational techniques allow the parametric process to mimic biological reproductive techniques – the growth of a tree, the formation of a bud or a flower – to produce an elegant approximation of a natural form. This computer-generated landscape can comprise hundreds of thousands of iterations before it comes to its final resolution. The result of the process in this instance means that the crematorium's undulating concrete roof is a continuation of the building, with a cogent structural logic of its own that sits apparently instinctively within its context, rather than being an indulgent addition. It is a truly impressive structural resolution – at various points the roof is only 20 centimetres (7 inches) deep.

The roof is supported at twelve points where it elegantly joins the slender, fluted conical columns that contain the hidden roof drainage run-offs. Extending beyond the sides of the building beneath, the roof also acts as shelter to the external areas, providing cover for the visitor parking that serves the crematorium. The various convex and concave curves in the roof correspond with the functions below – the private dining rooms, ceremonial spaces and cremation areas – which are enclosed in more conventional box-like rooms. The echoing of the external environment is maintained within, where the glazing offers expansive views of the countryside outside. Floor-to-ceiling windows with minimal detailing blur the lines between inside and out and make the marble-floored lobby areas feel part of the park outside. At night the interior becomes a beacon, with light shining through the glazing, shaped by the sweeping profile of the roof above.

MEISO NO MORI MUNICIPAL FUNERAL HALL
Toyo Ito & Associates | Kakamigahara, Gifu, Japan, 2006

Intended to evoke the lightness of a cloud and reflect the natural beauty of the site, this crematorium emulates a new landscape, replacing an existing building on the site that had fallen into disrepair.

2

The roof landscape was created with advanced parametric techniques that mimic biological reproductive techniques – the growth of trees, or a flower bud – to approximate a natural form.

MEISO NO MORI MUNICIPAL FUNERAL HALL   *Toyo Ito & Associates*

3
At points only 20 cm (8 in) deep, the roof is supported by twelve fluted conical columns that elegantly join the roof and contain the roof drainage.

4
Though light and thin, the reinforced concrete roof shell belies its strength: it can support the weight of people walking upon the surface.

5
Floor plan: Within the sinuous external envelope, interior functions of the crematorium are organised in traditional orthogonal volumes, with private ceremonial functions arranged furthest from lakeside views.

6
Section: The convex and concave curves in the roof correspond with the functions below, articulating places for ceremony, cremation and private dining.

5↑   6↓

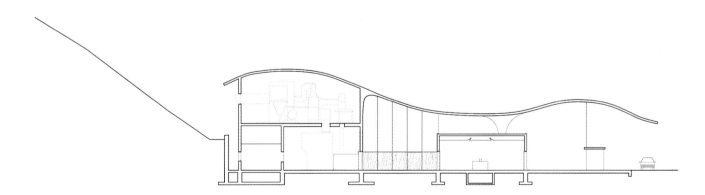

←7 8↑ 9↓

7
Floor-to-ceiling windows with minimal detailing blur the distinction between inside and out, making the marble-floored lobby areas feel like an extension of the park.

8
A view to the lake from one of the assembly rooms shows the curved profile that is representative of the structure of each of the twelve supporting columns.

9
The undulating roof line also articulates the interior ceiling. Soft, indirect lighting illuminates the curved geometry and is reflected on the highly polished stone. At night, the interior glows like a beacon.

Thanks in part to the Islamic faith's belief that mankind and animals should not be represented in figurative art in a religious context, the decoration of the majority of both traditional and contemporary mosques involves the use of abstract and decorative pattern, and we have come to be familiar with richly patterned mosques as the norm. In this project in the suburbs of the busy Bangladesh port city of Chittagong, architect Kashef Chowdhury of URBANA has shunned a noisy decorative style and created a calm and contemporary mosque that uses a minimalist design vocabulary to create an understated place of serenity.

Chowdhury was born in Dhaka, Bangladesh, the son of a civil engineer, and graduated in architecture from the Bangladesh University of Engineering and Technology before attending the Glenn Murcutt Master Class in Sydney, Australia. In his practice, he insists on a simplicity of approach to create buildings that work in concordance with nature. Writing in the *Architectural Review,* critic Catherine Slessor described the way in which, until recently, such was Chowdhury's respect for time, that he deliberately resisted using any artificial light in his studio, forcing him and his staff to work within daylight hours, helping to cre-

ate a natural pattern to the working day and discouraging working excessively long hours. This purity of approach and desire to bring the outside elements into his buildings is reflected in the design of the Chandgaon Mosque. As well as using minimal surface decoration, the functional spaces have been stripped back to the minimum. This typological back-to-basics approach took the practice of mosque-building, which has developed over a millennium and a half, and pared it down to a contemporary reading of what its fundaments should be. The mosque is intended to be both a meeting place for the community and a place of worship. These are the two essential elements that are simply expressed in the monolithic and spare mosque, simplified to simple geometries.

Once inside the complex, which is separated from the surrounding scrub land by a low white wall, a sloping path leads the faithful to two identical square volumes that sit squatly within the tree-lined boundaries of the site. The cuboid volumes lack any ornamental detail and only the large rectangular apertures that allow exterior views break their plain, whitewashed facades. These two blocks are identical in size and both have heavy masonry walls. The

eastern volume is punctuated by low, wide openings on to the surrounding landscape and accommodates a courtyard gathering space, dominated by a large glazed oculus that opens the space to the elements. The light thrown by this oculus moves across the interior as the sun moves through the sky, tracking the passage of time between prayer sessions over the white walls and stone floors.

The western block accommodates the prayer space. Here, the circular language set up by the oculus in the courtyard is repeated, but in this case features a dome, whose large aperture allows indirect light into the room, illuminating the mihrab wall. In both the spaces, supporting columns are kept to the perimeter of each volume, creating a sort of interior cloister, the large span allowing for the uninterrupted gathering of a large number of worshippers. While the apertures give a sense of openness and draw in light and ventilation by day, by night they allow light to shine out of the mosque, creating the effect of a lantern. Marble flooring helps cool the space and gives a sense of understated opulence that evokes tradition without stooping to pastiche.

CHANDGAON MOSQUE
Kashef Chowdhury | URBANA | Chittagong, Bangladesh, 2007

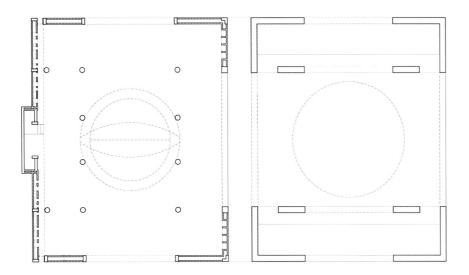

3↑ 4↓

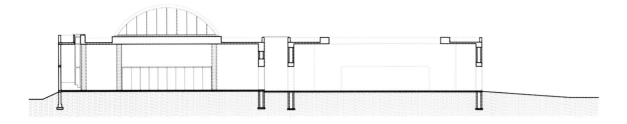

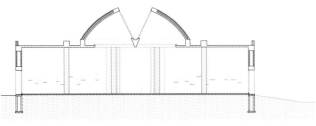

5↑ 6↓ 7→

1
This mosque on the suburban periphery of the port of Chittagong in Bangladesh seeks to fulfil the traditional role of a mosque as both a place of spirituality and as a gathering place for the community.

2
The eastern volume is punctuated by wide, low openings to the surrounding landscape and is dominated by a large oculus that opens the space to the elements, tracking the passage of time between prayer sessions as the sun passes overhead.

3
Floor plan: Both eastern and western volumes are essential rectilinear spaces in which supporting columns are restricted to the perimeter, creating an expansive interior cloister in each.

4
Long section: Mirroring each other in height and materiality, the arched aperture of the western volume houses a sheltered prayer hall and provides a counterpoint to the eastern volume, which is arranged as an open court.

5
Cross-section: The roof apertures give a sense of openness and draw in light and ventilation by day; by night they allow light to shine out of the mosque like a lantern.

6
This contemporary interpretation of a millennium-old architectural tradition has resulted in a monolithic and spare mosque, pared down to two identical cuboid structures constructed from white-washed masonry with accents of cool white marble.

7
A sheltered courtyard adjacent the eastern volume includes planting and a small pond, which aids cooling and references vegetation of surrounding scrub lands.

8
Though visually connected, the mosque is separated from its surroundings by a low white-washed wall that echoes the spartan materiality of the complex.

9
The mosque's subdued aesthetic synthesizes with the building's function. Rather than choosing to follow the traditional, highly decorative mosque canon, the architects endeavoured to incorporate all the essential elements of a mosque in a simple, clean design.

10
Detail view of the semi-domed rooflights in the western volume, which illuminates the mihrab wall.

11
In the front court, heavy masonry walls are punctuated with low, wide openings onto the surrounding landscape, and a large eye-like roof opening.

8↑ 9↓ 10↘

.1↑

British designer John Pawson came to prominence in the 1990s with a series of projects that drew upon the most austere, stripped-back Modernism of Mies van der Rohe. Updating it for a new set of clients like Calvin Klein, this new type of Minimalism reduced its colour palette and took influences from Japanese Zen philosophy to complement the reworking of classical Modernism.

One of his most successful and famous works was the 2004 Nový Dvůr abbey for Cistercian monks in the Czech Republic, on a 100-hectare (247-acre) estate west of Prague, near Touzim. The monks asked Pawson to work for them, despite their – now famous – reservations that his work was too austere even for their ascetic tastes.

Pawson's latest liturgical work is the interior modelling of the St Moritz Church in Augsburg, one of the largest cities in the Southern German state of Bavaria, and was completed in 2013. The church's elders approached Pawson after having seen his work at Nový Dvůr, and admiring the way in which he developed an atmosphere of serenity and contemplation with a palette of virtually all white, a judicious control of lighting and immaculate detailing. The church of St Moritz has stood since the days of the Holy Ro-man Empire and has been through many different costume changes and makeovers during its thousand-year-plus lifespan. Originally built as a Romanesque basilica, it was reworked in the Gothic and then Baroque styles. The Allied bombing campaigns during World War II left only its walls standing and after 1945 it was rebuilt in a more plain fashion by architect Dominikus Böhm, who gave the church an austere makeover, a restraint that foreshadowed characteristics of Pawson's work which was to come later. However, over the years the church gathered an accretion of extra layers of furniture and fittings, leading to the parish commissioning an artist, Juliane Stiegele, to create an artwork that would reinstate visual peace to the church. Her piece, *Void*, which she likened to a 'visual fast', removed any non-essential fitting or furniture, laying the groundwork for Pawson's permanent renovation.

Pawson's approach was to pare back the church to its fundamentals and span the generations by creating an architecture that respects its past while creating something new, functional and appropriate. The main focus of the work, as is often the case in Pawson's architecture, was that of subtraction and clarification, retaining much of the structure but stripping back ornamentation and radically manipulating the way in which light is used throughout.

Laminated onyx panels on the apse windows give a diffuse, ethereal light to the church. After dusk, concealed LED light fittings in the apse and nave gradually fill the church with a yellowish light. The only colours that deviate from the church's minimalist palette are the light beige Portuguese limestone used for the altar and the floor and the dark-stained wood that is used for pews, altar stalls and the organ surround.

After the second Vatican Council of 1965, Roman Catholic doctrine changed, so when Böhm reworked the church the priests still said mass with their backs to the congregation. Accordingly, Pawson brought the altar forward, bringing the liturgy closer to the congregation and making it possible to put the principal liturgical landmarks – the altar, the ambo and the sedilia – on a single level. The nods to the Baroque history in the form of the conserved statues of the apostles and the figure of Christ the Saviour, help contribute to the charged atmosphere of a church that one would struggle to call homely or welcoming, but packs a powerful spiritual and aesthetic punch.

ST MORITZ CHURCH

John Pawson | Augsburg, Bavaria, Germany, 2013

1↓ 2→

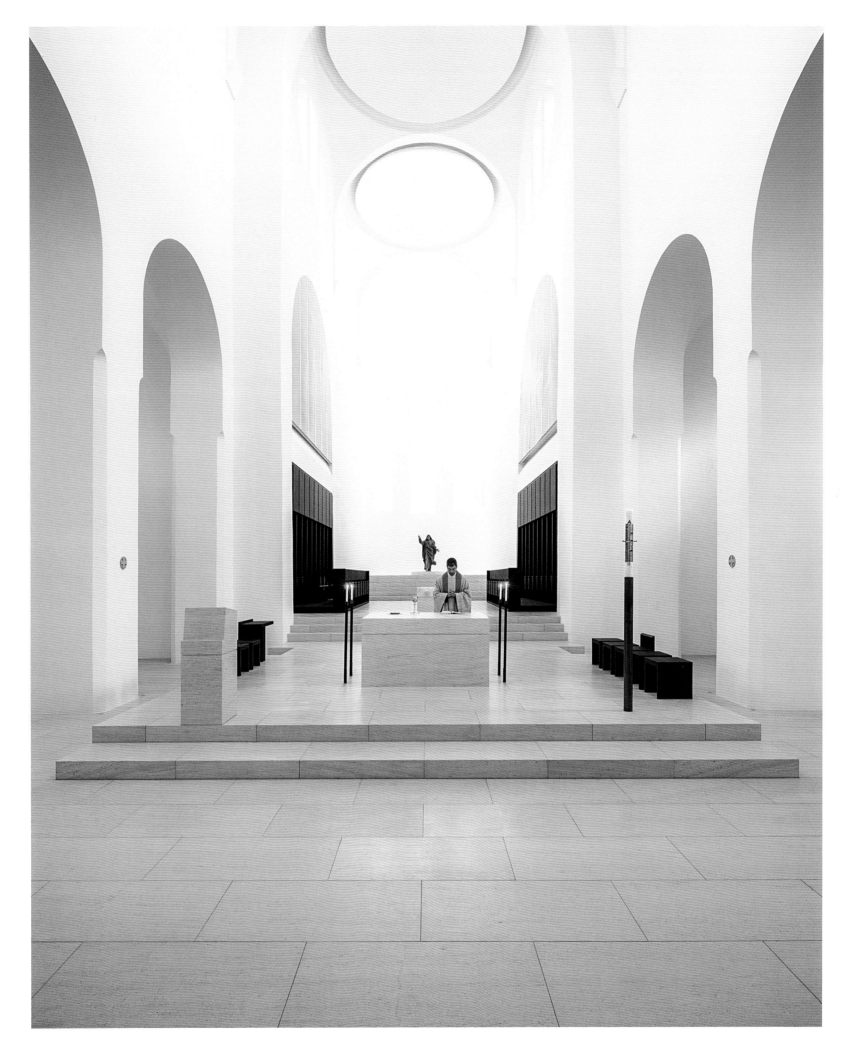

ST MORITZ CHURCH **John Pawson**

1
Pawson's main approach was to strip back ornamentation and radically manipulate the way light is used. Laminated onyx panels of the apse windows introduce a diffuse, ethereal light to the interior.

2
The minimal palette of white that articulates the volume of this church – and much of Pawson's work – is only deviated from with the pale beige Portuguese limestone of the altar and the floor.

3
Dark-stained timber of pews, altar stalls, doors and the organ surround contrast strongly with the white-washed walls.

4
Floor plan: Extant since the Holy Roman Empire, and originally built as a Romanesque basilica, the church was reworked in Gothic and Baroque styles before bombing during World War II left just two walls standing. It was then rebuilt in an austere fashion by architect Dominikus Böhm.

5
Section: Recognizing the change to Roman Catholic doctrine in 1965, Pawson brought the altar further up the nave, bringing the liturgy closer to the congregation and uniting the principal liturgical landmarks of altar, ambo and sedilia, on a single level.

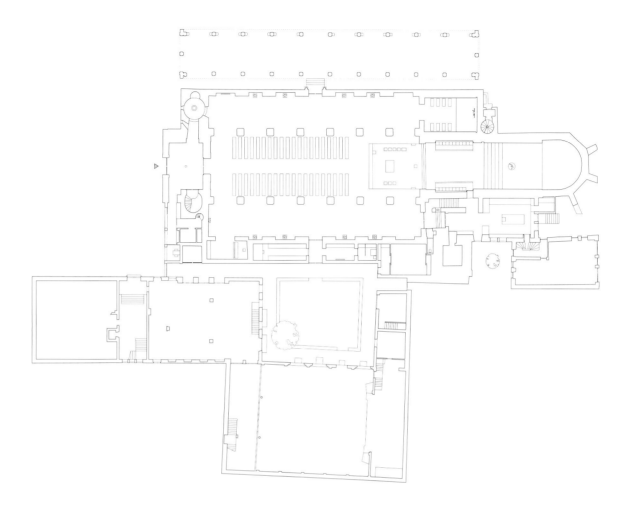

←3   4↑   5↓

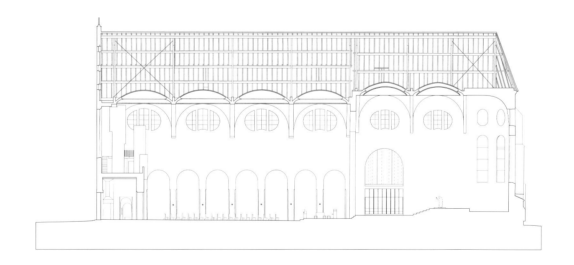

6
Pawson's approach to pare back the church to its fundaments creates an austere sense of order and a spartan canvas for decorative elements, such as the crucifix in the chapel, which concludes the left aisle.

7
Traces of the church's Baroque history are seen in the spatial organization, the shape of windows, and in the restored carved figures of the apostles positioned in recessed niches of the aisles.

8
A wooden sculpture of Christ the Saviour by Baroque sculptor, Georg Petel, is the focal point of the apse. Raised on a series of steps, it is highlighted by natural light filtered through the onyx windows.

9
Lighting of the church is strongest in the nave and apse, where services are performed and the congregation gathers under Böhm's original calottes. The aisles have more subdued lighting.

ST MORITZ CHURCH   John Pawson

When Jun Aoki took on the project to build a wedding chapel within the grounds of the Hyatt Regency hotel in Osaka, Japan, it was clear that there would be plenty of opportunity to use the symbolism of water to help create an atmosphere for lovers, young and old, to celebrate their marriages. The waterfront hotel was built on land reclaimed from the sea and extensive pools and lakes were part of its landscape design. Aoki's chapel is a one-storey glass lozenge, with an irregular seven-sided polygon plan, that appears to sit upon a lake. Thanks, in part, to its combination of blank and patterned elevations, its scale is deceptive. One would not necessarily realize that inside there was a triple-height space that helps amplify the significance and seriousness of the wedding ceremonies within.

The tone of luxury, appropriate to the high-end hotel chain of which it is part, and the significance of the building's function, is set up by the use of white marble as the cladding on all but two of its sides. The remaining walls, which look out on to the lake, are clad with floor-to-ceiling glass. Behind the glass wall is a screen made of stainless steel rings arranged in a truncated tetrahedron. This

structure supports the roof on one of the longer sides of the chapel and articulates the second theme that complements the water: the use of diffuse light to create a serene and beautiful atmosphere within the chapel. While the stacked rings can be viewed from outside the chapel, creating a pattern that animates the large, otherwise blank facades, from inside one does not get a direct view of them. Layers of diaphanous, semi-transparent fabric are hung in front of the screen, muting the rings' presence – rather than projecting a stark silhouette, they reveal a dappled pattern that slowly shifts as the curtains move in the breeze. This also results in the space being flooded with natural light, but this is sufficiently diffused by the screens and curtain so as not to be distracting. Shadows cast by the rings on the facing walls help enrich the atmosphere of an otherwise plainly decorated room.

The screen comprises one of the hidden thresholds, a theme which runs throughout the project. The chapel is hidden from public view, with the congregation entering it by accessing the hotel and going through its gardens. A bridge takes the congregants, bride and groom

over a pond and into the interior of the chapel. The chapel building itself is subdivided into three spaces: the covered entry porch space, located at one of the buildings' apexes, where the pathways meet the chapel and the congregation can gather before a ceremony; the adjoining foyer space, in the middle of the polygon and equipped with storage cupboards on each side; and at the apex the chapel, which projects into the lake.

Once visitors pass into the chapel, they enter a much larger volume than the sequence they have been through on their journey to that point. The chapel opens up to a generous 6 metre (20 foot) floor-to-ceiling height. Eighteen pews – simple timber and steel constructions – provide a coloured counterpoint to the predominantly white furnishings and the marble floors. The chapel tapers to a point towards its rear, focusing the congregation's view to the area in which the celebrant stands with a hardwood lectern in front and a tall timber cross behind – the only signs of any religious iconography in the building.

WHITE CHAPEL
Jun Aoki & Associates | Osaka, Japan, 2006

1↓   2→

WHITE CHAPEL **Jun Aoki & Associates**

1

Proceedings in the wedding chapel of Osaka's Park Hyatt are screened from view behind glazed walls that enclose a matrix of stainless steel rings. White marble that befits the luxury hotel is used to clad the remaining five walls.

2

Built on land reclaimed from the sea, the tetrahedron of the wedding chapel appears to float on the lake, drawing on the poetic symbolism associated with water to create an appropriate atmosphere for celebrating marriage.

3

Section: From a sheltered entry porch, visitors follow a processional sequence, leading them from a covered entry porch, through a more compressed foyer space into the generous triple-height chapel.

4

Floor plan: The chapel is formed as an irregular seven-sided polygon and is accessed from the hotel gardens via two bridges.

5

At night the chapel glows like an illuminated lozenge, its diffuse interior light casting dramatic patterned reflections on the surface of the water.

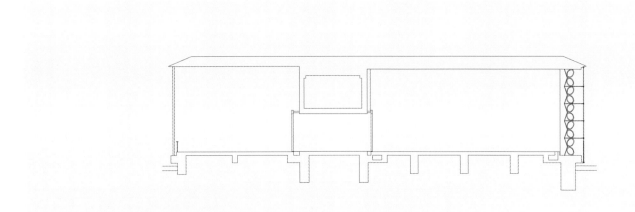

3 ↑   4 ↓   5 →

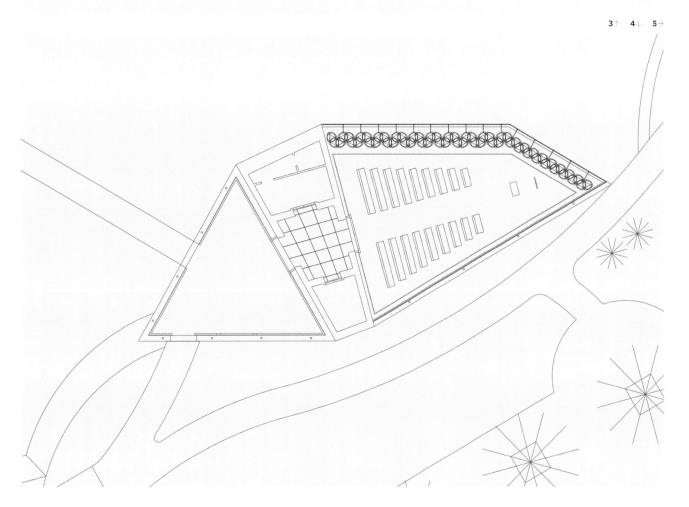

6
The surprisingly large and irregular volume of the chapel is predominantly furnished in white, with marble floors. Its eighteen steel and timber pews, and the hardwood lectern and cross are the only counterpoint to the ethereal space.

7
Supporting the length of roof on the longer side of the chapel, the screen of stainless steel rings also filters and diffuses natural light to the interior. Lengths of diaphanous semi-transparent fabric hang inside the chapel to soften the presence of the rings, which appear as a changing dappled pattern from within.

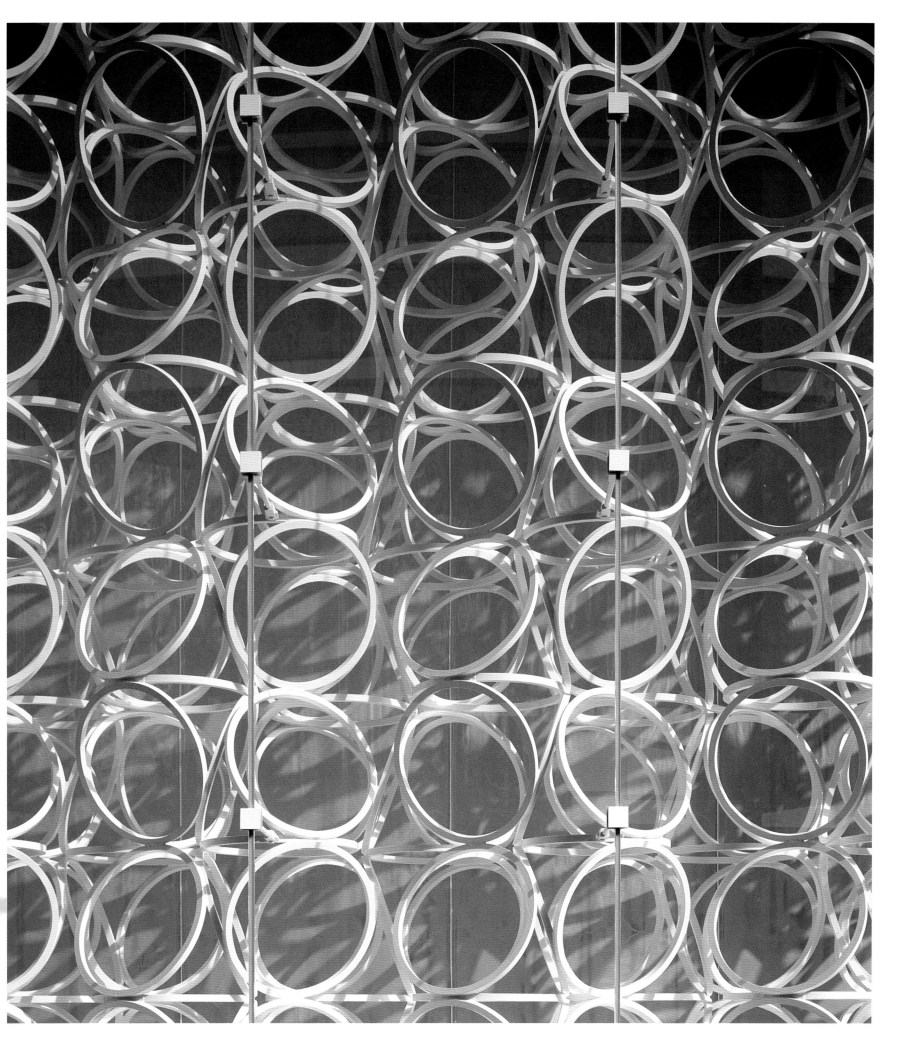

Borrowing heavily from the agricultural language of the buildings that make up its neighbours, this modest contemporary version of a French barn is the first newly built Buddhist meditation centre of its kind in The Netherlands. Despite interest in the religion shown by a smattering of nineteenth-century intellectuals like Friedrich Nietzsche and Arthur Schopenhauer, Buddhism historically failed to make much headway as a dominant faith in Europe. The last decade has seen it become one of Europe's fastest growing religions, but its numbers remain small, with an estimated three to four million Buddhists in a European population of over seven hundred million.

Named the 'Metta Vihara', which translates roughly as 'community of loving kindness', the centre belongs to the Triratna Community of Buddhists and is intended for use as a meditation centre and place of retreat from the stresses, tensions and distractions of everyday modern life. Its rural location gives it an isolation that helps with this programme, situated as it is in the small rural village of Hengstdijk in a remote southern part of the Netherlands, close to the country's border with Belgium. The place of retreat is a commonplace element of many faiths, yet most

European examples of the form take their influence from Christian monastic buildings.

This long building has twenty-six beds split between thirteen one- and two-person bedrooms on the first storey, with social spaces – a meditation hall, library, kitchen and dining hall – on the ground floor. The brief was to create a building that while beautiful, was not overly comfortable. For Buddhists, relaxation is an important element of being on retreat, but not to the extent that one would be as relaxed as in one's own home – creature comforts should be limited. There was also a requirement to keep costs to a minimum. The centre is financed mainly through gifts from members and friends of the community so excessive spending was not a possibility. All these factors, together with the agricultural context, meant that an adaptation of the mansard barn structure, built with corrugated sheeting and a timber frame, was the ideal solution for reasons of appearance, cost and situation.

In section, the barn is of a classic mansard shape. Three horizontal bands, delineated by the timber lines of the beams and the alternating colour in the corrugated metal, make up the elevations, with two further bands

on the pitched roof. Instead of developing a complicated detail to overcome the tricky nature of joining corrugated sheet metal, white timber window frames were used at each end of the steel sheet. Standard Velux window units were chosen for their relatively low cost and good insulation. Together with the windows, the two-tone corrugated sheet used to cover the building breaks up its mass and helps it blend in to the hues of the surrounding landscape.

Contrasting with the steel, the ends of the building are clad in timber, again to cut costs – the team used offcuts and waste pieces of wood taken from the builder's supplies. Inside the building, a simple and austere palette of modest and unfinished materials has been used. The floors are polished concrete, aside from those in the meditation hall, which has black bamboo flooring. Two large French doors open up the meditation hall to the landscape outside, while large corrugated steel barn doors outside the French doors shade the space from the sunlight. On the other side of the building's long elevation, a series of pilotis support the first storey, creating a covered walkway in which to sit and look out in contemplation at the surrounding fields.

BUDDHIST MEDITATION CENTRE METTA VIHARA

bureau SLA | Hengstdijk, The Netherlands, 2012

1↓   2→

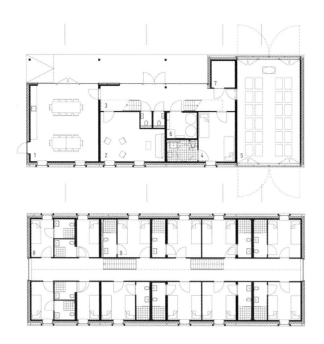

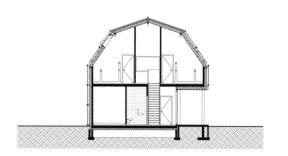

1
Borrowing from the agricultural language of neighbouring buildings, this Buddhist meditation centre is a modest contemporary version of a French barn.

2
Simple and inexpensive materials are used throughout the centre, including corrugated sheeting in two tones, offcuts from builder's supplies for the timber ends, and standard Velux windows.

3
Ground and first floor plans: Accommodation for twenty-six people is arranged in one- and two-person bedrooms on the first floor. The meditation hall, library, kitchen and dining hall are at ground level.

4
Section: Formed in a classic mansard shape, the agricultural barn typology of the Buddhist centre was the ideal solution to a restricted budget and an appearance appropriate to the rural location.

5
Two large, operable French doors open the meditation hall to the meadow beyond. The hall can be protected from direct sunlight by large corrugated steel barn doors.

6
Each elevation is composed of three horizontal bands delineated by timber beams and alternating coloured corrugated metal. This reduces the mass of the building and responds to hues of the surrounding landscape.

7↑ 8↓ 9→

7
A simple colour palette of white-washed walls and polished concrete floors is found in all ground level spaces, apart from the meditation hall, which has black bamboo flooring.

8
Bedrooms are appropriately austere spaces for relaxation and retreat. Standard materials such as the Velux windows in each room were chosen for their relatively low cost and good insulation.

9
A series of pilotis on one of the building's long elevations supports the first storey and creates a covered walkway adjacent to the internal social spaces from which to contemplate the surrounding fields.

The volcanic Jeju Island is a popular destination for Korean couples to go on honeymoon, drawn in by its warm climes, tropical beaches and historically risqué reputation as a destination for Korean newlyweds. Its bevy of eccentric museums includes a park of erotic sculptures as well as the Trick Art Museum, where optical illusions and tromp l'oeil are used to rework Old Masters paintings, to the delight of selfie-snapping tourists. Nearby, at the southwest of the island, is the significantly more sober Biotopia housing complex by Japanese practice Itami Jun Architects, part of the expansion of the Seojopu district. This low-lying cluster of over one hundred residential units is set in a rolling landscape, on a site that had suffered from degraded soil conditions and required rehabilitation. The project took its inspiration from a project in Germany that made rejuvenation and soil remediation of a former brownfield site central to its landscaping strategy. As part of these residential clusters, Itami Jun Architects also built four cultural buildings, the Water, Wind, Stone and Land art galleries. The Church of Water and Light adds to this civic ensemble and similarly aims to sit calmly within its landscape.

The church is a long building, with a pitched roof, slung low across its footprint, that doesn't interrupt the views of the gently rolling hills that surround it. The pitched roof has a distinctive tiling pattern which is made up of triangular tiles in different shades of teal, greys and blues. These were chosen by the architect as a means of echoing the dappled light caused by the sun piercing nearby trees and the constantly changing skies experienced above the tropical island. The Tokyo-based practice describe trying to create a 'sky architecture' in their structure, one that would reflect and not work against the spectacular and often changing skies of the locale.

Another starting point for the architects was the theme of a boat upon water. This evolved into the approach of having the church surrounded by a small moat, out of which the walls appear to rise. The church is accessed by walkways that cross the water, both at the rear of the church and at the middle. One side is a cloistered walkway that runs the length of the building, and through glass windows, brings light into the building's lobby and mediates between inside and out. The Church of Water and Light

is characterised by an intriguing mix of traditional formal approaches and materials with more contemporary tropes in the materiality and detailing. This is most obviously articulated in the roof with its bright patterned tiles, as well as its structure. The church deviates from the classic form of the long barn by a gable end that is larger in section at the end than it is at the middle, thus creating a sort of contemporary hipped barn that expands towards its end. In the middle is a chamfered chimney stack. This mix of traditional and new is also expressed in the structure. While timber is used to clad the church, the structure is of a steel frame made of square sections. The columns and beams were then wrapped in a wood veneer. The interiors are also timber lined, and the main part of the church is given over to a nave that runs the width of the barn, top lit by a lantern providing a dim light and atmospheric mood. The church was built using a high quality specification for materials, detailing and construction and is hoped to be a lasting and durable addition to the Seojopu new town.

CHURCH OF WATER AND LIGHT
Itami Jun Architects | Seojopu, Jeju Island, South Korea, 2009

1↓   2→

CHURCH OF WATER AND LIGHT Itami Jun Architects

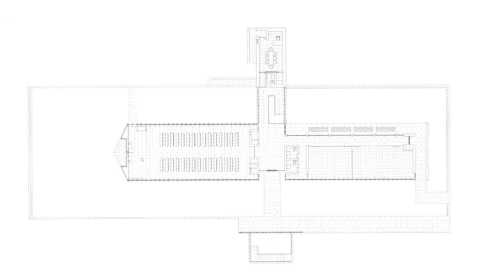

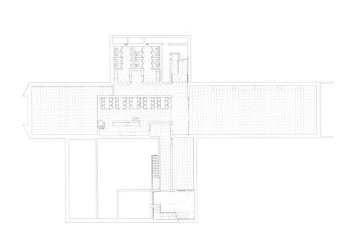

Surrounded by a small moat, the church is thought of as a boat upon water. Drawing a biblical analogy, it is accessed by walkways that cross the shallow pond.

2

A steeply pitched, glazed gable that is larger in section than the rest of the building differentiates the church from usual barn typology. The expansive wall contains a nave that occupies the full width and admits natural light within.

3

The long, low building sits calmly within the landscape and allows views to the gently rolling hills that surround it. A cloistered walkway runs the length of one elevation, introducing light to the interior and mediating between inside and out.

4

Ground floor plan: Arranged in a cruciform shape, visitors enter the church at the central point beneath a chamfered chimney: the space for worship occupies the large raked space (left) while parish offices are contained in the lower volume facing it (right).

5

Lower floor plan: Accessed from the central stairwell, ancillary areas below ground house a large refectory, kitchen, pantry, installations and a parish hall.

6

The pitched roof has a distinctive tiling pattern that is composed of triangular tiles in different shades of teal, greys, and blues, which recall the dappled light of sunshine in tree canopies nearby.

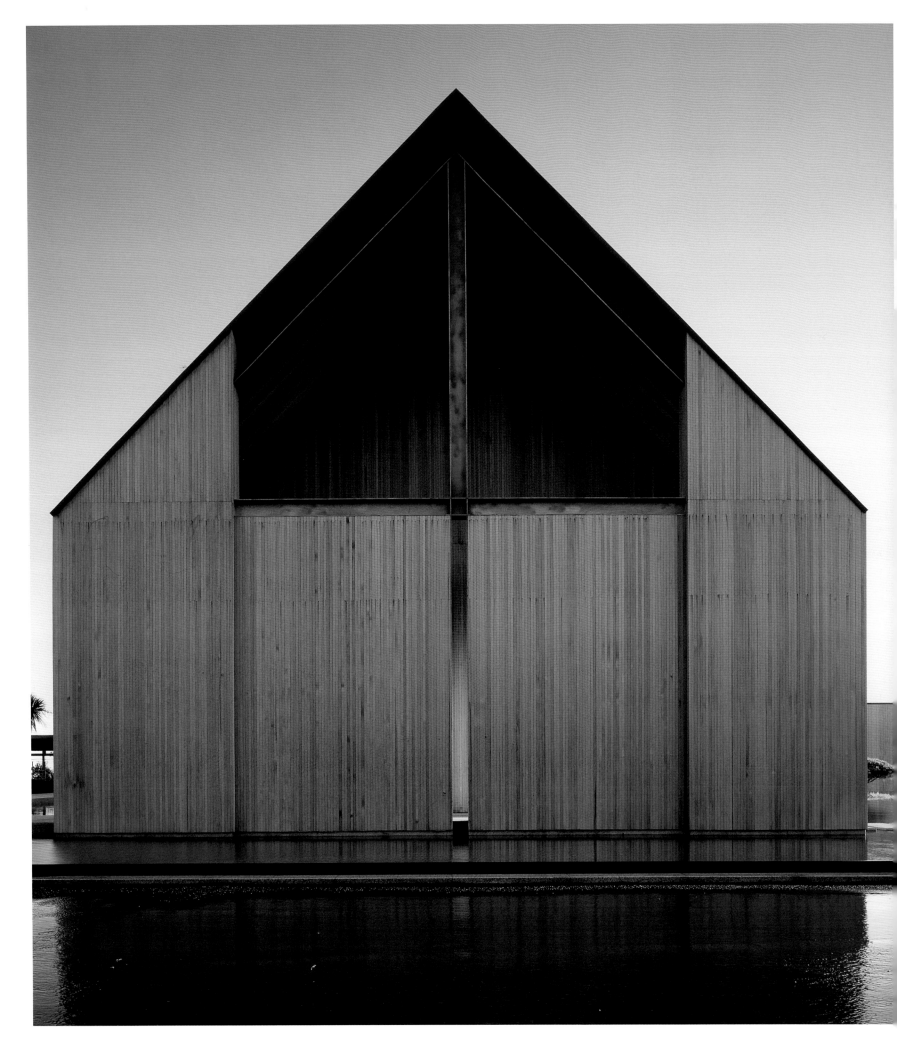

7

A mix of traditional and new is expressed in the church structure, which is predominantly clad in timber but is formed of a steel frame of square sections. One elevation uses the exposed square steel sections to reveal a subtle cruciform motif.

8

The nave is top lit by a lantern cut into a metal screen, that also mediates natural light from the opaque windows. All interiors are lined in timber to create a subdued atmosphere for worship.

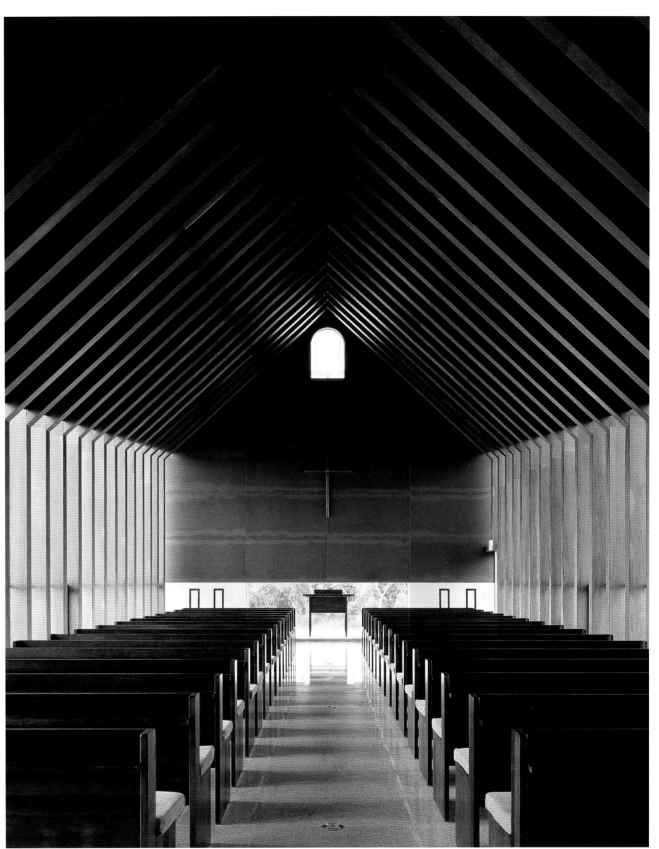

←**7**   **8**↑

MASS

MASS

Solidity, permanence and stability: these are some of the things which religion has offered generations of believers, and the buildings they build to worship in often articulate these characteristics. With the developments in industry and agriculture over the last three centuries, a large segment of the world's population is enjoying a hitherto unimaginable prosperity. From this perspective it can sometimes be difficult to envisage the extent of the uncertainties that faced our ancestors, whether that be infant mortality, violent death, plague, or unpredictable harvests. Thanks to scientific advances, many of these are no longer everyday concerns for a significant proportion of the world's population. And even with the advantages of technological know-how and relative prosperity, life can and does sometimes deal us an unexpected cruel hand.

It makes sense, then, that many religious buildings express their authority and function through an imposing presence of permanence. The thick walls of a Romanesque church suggest security; the vaulting ceiling of a Gothic cathedral an awesome exercise in transcendence, as well as a display of wealth and power; the travertine floor of a mosque suggests an opulence that comes about through a communal devotion to a higher power. As well as certainty and heaviness, there is also the need to invoke the sometimes opposing feelings of ambiguity, levity and divinity, and it is when these factors are combined that the effect of religious architecture is at its greatest. The following examples display both this certainty and levity, but are also remarkable for the ingenuity with which they deploy and deal with depth, weight, solidity and mass. At Stanley Saitowitz's Beth Sholom Synagogue in San Francisco (page 108), the sanctuary is elevated above street level, a large curved, masonry-fronted volume that visitors have to climb steps to reach. Here the solid mass of the sanctuary reminds us of the importance of the physical temple, and its destruction and ultimate restoration, to the Jewish faith.

There are many instances in Judaeo-Christian scripture of topographic and geological significance, whose imagery can be symbolized in religious buildings: Moses went up the mountain for counsel; the Ten Commandments were inscribed on tablets of stone; the First and Second Temples at Jerusalem were torn down. In the New Testament, the disciple Peter was to be the rock upon which Jesus Christ built his church, and it was in a cave-like tomb that he was buried. This is the language of robust elements, mass, weight and volume, rather than filigree and finesse, or to borrow the language of critic Kenneth Frampton, the building of stereotomics, rather than tectonics. The Rituals Crematorium by

+udeb arquitectos (page 114) is an example of this, a building that rises from the hillside, standing proud like the plug of a volcano, which has remained after its more porous slopes have been eroded away. The uncompromising nature of the large orthogonal volume of the main temple at the Rituals Crematorium is mitigated and balanced by a sequence of pathways and squares which take mourners along a carefully choreographed journey from their arrival point. The solidity of the building may offer mourners some brief solace, a reassuring permanence in the face of loss. While their loved ones will soon go back to dust, the building will remain long after they themselves return back to the earth.
In the Netherlands, Claus van Wageningen's Dutch Reformed Church (page 120) presents an austere series of squat volumes to the street that enclose the liturgy rooms and meeting halls. Its formal language fits with the Modernist grid of its neighbourhood, and the lack of adornment is in keeping with the theology of its church – Protestantism that values simplicity and clarity.

Peter Zumthor's Brother Klaus Field Chapel (page 126) was dedicated to the patron saint of Switzerland, a peasant farmer who became a hermit and, according to folklore, retreated from his relatively untroubled life to live in a small cave. The chapel that Zumthor has built is a challenging, almost oppressive space. Its walls slope upwards to a narrow opening in the roof, leaving the visitor very aware of the weight and presence of the concrete that presses in around him. It's an uncompromising, yet strangely comforting, reminder of the ascetic life the saint chose to live.

The LJG Synagogue by SeARCH (page 132), also in the Netherlands, announces its presence to the street with its concrete cladding, arranged to form a Star of David. The building plays with light and space, through the large void cut into the building's long, rectilinear form. One of the enduring comforts which buildings of all types and sizes can offer is that these constructions will last long after our deaths, and often existed long before our births: they link us to generations past and future. This is particularly true of religious buildings, whose associated communities often emphasize being part of a continuum of people who will be united in the afterlife. In the meantime, we will all, at our own prescribed time, return to the ground, 'ashes to ashes and dust to dust'. These buildings remain however, and in their own, fathomable, earthbound way, offer us some sort of continuity. And even if these buildings last a thousand years, a blink in the eye in terms of geological timescales, this is an immortality of sorts.

The tent and the temple. These two contrasting building types, both integral to the story of the Jewish people, are neatly expressed in the formal language of the Ohel Jakob Synagogue on Sankt-Jakobs-Platz in Munich, Germany. The synagogue is the centrepiece of a complex of three buildings that forms part of, and sits within, a series of new public spaces.

In elevation, the synagogue can be divided into two parts – firstly, a squat base of rough-faced travertine and secondly a glazed lantern superstructure that sits on top of it. The glass- and steel-framed lantern, screened with filigree metal mesh, invokes the tent – or tabernacle – that in the Old Testament was erected by Moses, under God's instructions, while leading his people through the desert following their exodus from Egypt. Situated at the centre of the exiled Jews' encampment, a pillar of cloud was said to have appeared above the tabernacle during the day and a pillar of fire by night as a symbol of God's presence.

The synagogue's semi-transparent glass and steel volume, which similarly glows gently at night, contrasts dramatically with the massive travertine base from which it rises. For architects Wandel Hoefer Lorch, this heavily grounded

volume speaks of a later period in the Jews' history, that of the solidity of King Solomon's temple. Taken together the distinct structural elements of the synagogue articulate a charged tension – fragility versus stability, the provisional versus the permanent – that has an additional resonance given the irrevocably altered position of Gemany's Jewish community after World War II.

The Ohel Jakob Synagogue is also remarkable because it marks a new, more confident, phase in German-Jewish post-war history – it is the first monumental freestanding synagogue built in Germany since the late 1920s. Prior to 1938, large synagogues were commonly found in Germany, particularly in major cities, and as such were a familiar part of the urban landscape. The community facilities usually associated with these earlier synagogues were housed, if necessary, in outbuildings. After 1945, by contrast, the much-reduced size of the German-Jewish population meant that community facilities were focused into a single complex – to the detriment, from an architectural point of view, of the monumental impact of a Jewish synagogue, which depends upon its distance from the viewer to create an effect.

Here, the synagogue is the dominant player in the trio. Adjacent buildings host the ancillary community centre and museum. Its neighbours have adopted muted variations on the materials palette and formal language set up by the synagogue. The community centre and the museum both use polished travertine, while the museum – the smaller of the two ancillary buildings – inverts the dichotomous relationship set up by the synagogue, with glazing at ground-floor level and a travertine cube that hosts the exhibition space above.

The community centre has two underground floors and six upper floors, which house event rooms, dining facilities, a kindergarten, a library and offices. The museum has two exhibition spaces on its first and second floors, with a 200 square metre (2,150 square foot) permanent exhibition space at basement level. This complex of three complementary structures sets up a new set of public spaces and outdoor rooms. The succession of squares, pathways and passageways between them – the landscape design of the Sankt-Jakobs-Platz is by Office Regina Poly – helps weave this trio of buildings for the Jews of Munich back into the urban grain of the Bavarian capital.

JEWISH COMMUNITY CENTRE, SYNAGOGUE AND MUSEUM

Wandel Hoefer Lorch Architekten | Munich, Germany, 2007

1↓   2→

JEWISH COMMUNITY CENTRE, SYNAGOGUE AND MUSEUM   Wandel Hoefer Lorch Architekten

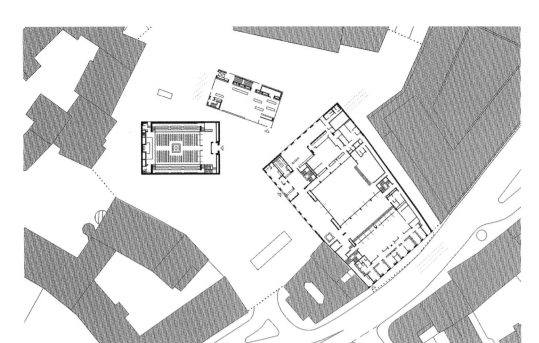

3↑ 4↓ 5↘

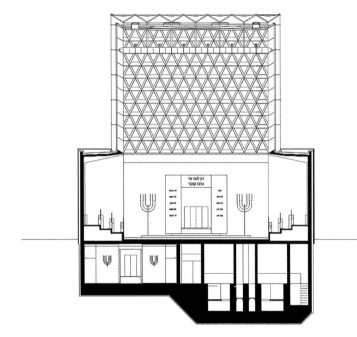

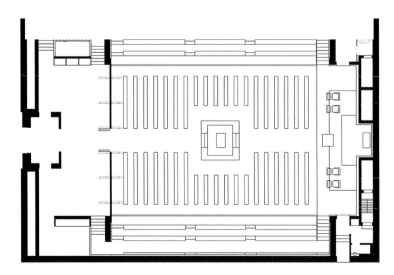

1
The rusticated elevations of the synagogue are composed of blank stone walls, apart from the elevation with the large entrance door. A bronze, triangular mesh system surrounds its steel and glass lantern structure, diffusing light and referencing the temporary materials of Moses's tabernacle.

2
A trio of buildings that make up the new complex at Sankt-Jakobs-Platz in Munich are united by muted variations of the materials palette and formal language of the synagogue.

3
Site plan: Sankt-Jakobs-Platz and surrounding streets contain the synagogue (left), community centre (centre) and museum (right) and create a new series of squares and pathways around the complex.

4
Ground floor plan: Reinstating the presence of large synagogues in Germany, the central space for worship is arranged in axial alignment. Supporting functions for the Jewish community are located in neighbouring buildings.

5
Section: The ideas of 'tent' and 'temple' that orchestrate the synagogue are illustrated through the filigree mesh of the glass and steel-framed lantern above a squat base of travertine.

6
Solar shading is provided by the diagrid structure of the metal mesh lantern cladding. When viewed from an oblique angle, the mesh resembles a honeycomb structure.

7
In contrast to the rough finish of the synagogue, polished travertine is used to clad the Jewish community centre and the museum.

6↓ 7→

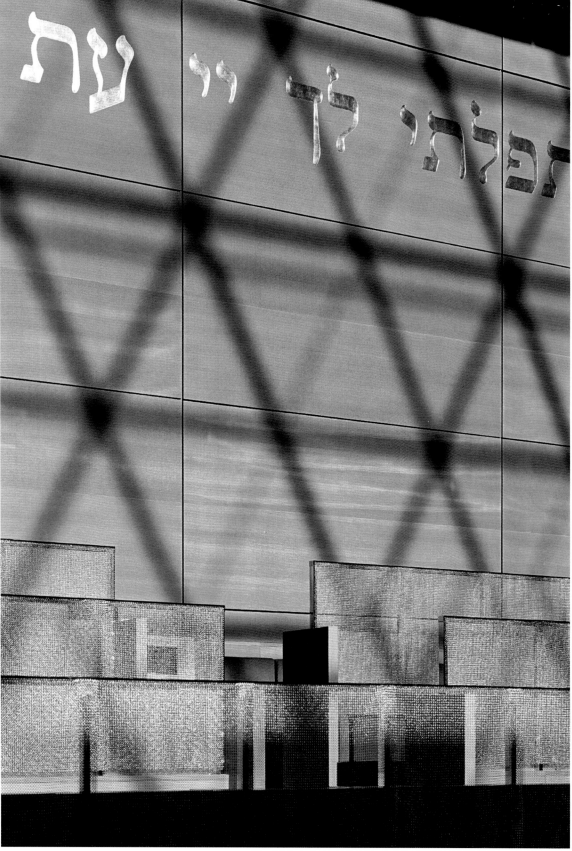

8↑ 9→

8
The triangular diagrid structure of the lantern casts shadows on the timber-lined interior of the synagogue that echo the Star of David motif.

9
From within, the glazed lantern provides fragmented views out over the historic streets of Munich. The apparent fragility of the steel and glass structure contrasts with the solidity the synagogue's body.

JEWISH COMMUNITY CENTRE, SYNAGOGUE AND MUSEUM Wandel Hoefer Lorch Architekten

At the intersection of two tree-lined San Francisco boulevards is the Beth Sholom Synagogue, the place of worship and community focal point for over 500 San Franciscan families who follow the so-called Conservative – or Masorti – strand of Judaism. This denomination, originating in nineteenth-century Germany, advocates the strict maintenance of Jewish tradition, and is distinct from Orthodox, Liberal or Reform Judaism. The community gained a larger plot to enable the expansion of its existing premises on 14th Avenue and Clement Street, close to Golden Gate and Presidio Parks and opposite the slightly overwrought neoclassical pomp of the Christian Science Church.

It is without doubt a striking building. The synagogue is made up of two structures: a masonry curvilinear form that sits above a low rectangular plinth, and a cube-like glass and zinc tower, which acts as the light and reflective foil to the mass and solidity of the sanctuary. The solid mass of the sanctuary reminds us of the importance of the physical temple – its destruction and its ultimate restoration – to the Jewish faith. Facing on to 14th Avenue, the primary place of worship, the sanctuary, sits within

a large honey-coloured inverted semicircle, which could pass for the underside of an ark, or a stylized silhouette of a menorah. The sanctuary sits on a one-storey plinth, which houses the daily chapel, meditation space, library, offices and meeting rooms. This then meets a cuboid block, the same height as the sanctuary, at the corner of the two streets. The glass-faced block of the social hall runs along the frontage of Clement Street. The final elements in this ensemble are the ground-floor courtyard between the social hall and the sanctuary hall and the courtyard at first-storey level from which the sanctuary is reached.

Many religions and religious buildings emphasize the importance of procession and here the walkway from street to sanctuary is well choreographed. Echoing the journey up the mountain Moses took to commune with God, visitors to the synagogue cross from the street into a lobby on the ground floor of the plinth building, then pass into an open courtyard. Stairs take them to another courtyard, this time at first-floor level, where they double back on themselves to ascend into the sanctuary itself, a ritual passage literally taking them closer to God.

Inside, the sacred sanctuary room, a space in the round, is focused on an understated central bimah from where the services are conducted. Unlike the Orthodox Jewish tradition, Conservative Jews worship together, with men and women participating equally in the liturgy, so the curtain or balcony separating men from women in some synagogues is not present here. The Beth Sholom Synagogue's seating arrangement consists of two sections of two-tiered, amphitheatre-style seats, facing one another across the sanctuary. Where one may expect open rooflights, an artificially lit soffit extends into the middle of the room, where it is pierced by glazing that runs down the centre of the sanctuary's axis. A slice of sky in the ceiling turns into the eternal light above the ark on the eastern wall. All light enters the room from above, with views of the sky creating a sense of sanctity and remove in the midst of the noise and bustle of the city. Through a linear rooflight in the ceiling this daylight floods the interior and along the edge of the eastern wall, creating menorah-like shadows from the six roof beam supports. At night, the room resembles the night sky with its constellation of ceiling lights.

BETH SHOLOM SYNAGOGUE

Stanley Saitowitz | **Natoma Architects** | San Francisco, California, USA, 2008

1↓   2→

BETH SHOLOM SYNAGOGUE Stanley Saitowitz – Natoma Architects

3↑ 4↓ 5↘

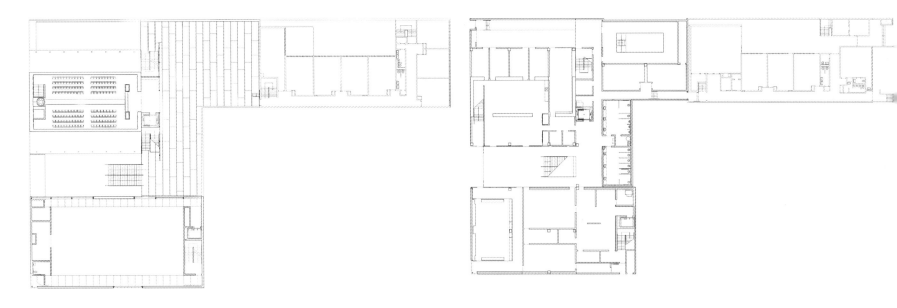

1

The synagogue is composed of two parts: a sanctuary hall and a social hall. The sanctuary is held in a pale golden masonry semi-circle that references a menorah and sits on a low plinth; a reflective cube-like tower of glass and zinc clads the social hall.

2

Entry to the sanctuary is carefully choreographed so visitors pass through the lobby in the plinth and enter a large courtyard between the social and sanctuary halls.

3

From the central courtyard, worshippers ascend a ceremonial staircase to reach the synagogue. This literallly and figuratively draws them closer to communion with God.

4

First floor plan: The sanctuary and social hall are accessed from a large open courtyard at the upper level.

5

Ground floor plan: A daily chapel, meditation space, library offices and meeting room are housed at street level.

6

Inside the sacred sanctuary room the space is focused on an understated central bimah from where services are conducted. Both men and women participate equally, negating the need for screening.

7

Section: Though composed of distinct forms and materials, both halls share an upper datum.

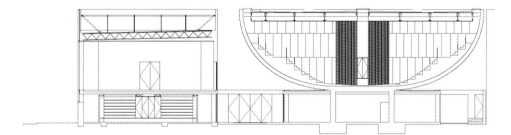

8
At street level the sanctuary appears like the underside of an ark. Procession from the entry up the first and subsequent flight of stairs is a reference to Moses's journey up the mountain to meet God.

9
Throughout the complex, ancillary rooms are lined in timber and have decorative panels, softening the atmosphere.

10
Six roof beam supports on the curved eastern wall of the sanctuary cast a shadow that recalls the shape of a menorah. All light in this sacred room falls from above to focus attention skyward and create visual and aural distance from the busy urban surroundings.

←8   9↑   10↓

In the hills of the Colombian department of Antioquia, is the town of Guarne, which lies to the north of the capital Bogotá and to the east of Medellín, the country's second largest city. Architect Felipe Uribe de Bedout and his practice +udeb have created a striking crematorium complex. A large, cuboid building rises out of the hillside, neighboured by a smaller, sculptural outpost, part of a complex interlinked by tunnels, bridges and a series of public and semi-public squares. The crematorium is reached via a bridge edged in Cor-Ten steel and paved with local stone, a materials palette which is used throughout for both buildings and landscape. This bridge crossing marks the first threshold that mourners pass over, a strong transitional marker in contrast with some of the softer thresholds elsewhere in the complex. Once over this cut in the landscape, the mourner walks up the pathway to a small square, which includes a seating area and space to gather, the back of which is defined by a large monolithic sculpture in Cor-Ten steel. Beneath this square is the crematorium building, which houses the furnaces and preparation rooms. This level is reached by a sloping ramp that takes the deceased from the car park in front of the moat to the basement of the crematorium building.

Mourners pass from this open square through a pathway cut into the sloped hillside to the principal building, the temple. Roughly square in plan, cuboid in mass, this is an imposing building with a reassuring solidity. Its otherwise windowless elevations, built in local stone, are broken up by T-sections of Cor-Ten casing, with the horizontal bar of the T making up the parapet of the facade. The gap established between the stone elevation and Cor-Ten parapet-cum-soffit is glazed, and allows illumination of the temple via light wells. On the elevation, these T-sections are placed asymmetrically, spaced out equally on all four sides. On the sides and rear of the building the bases of these Cor-Ten sections are glazed, letting some natural light into the building, which is largely artificially illuminated.

The temple is arranged around the central congregation space which has ten banks of pews oriented towards the lectern and the platform on which the deceased body lies. The pews are positioned at right angles to the axis set up by the entrance to the temple, which sits approximately southwest in orientation. Surrounding the gathering space are support and ancillary areas: on the front wall a staircase up to the first floor gallery and down to the basement, and on the back and side walls, private safes for storing ashes and the priest's office. On the first floor a balcony runs around the perimeter of the room, with space for a choir to gather above and to the rear of the congregation. Lights, hung from the roof in a grid that helps demarcate the place where the congregation sits, loom down to the level of the first storey, helping to create an intimate mood in what is actually a significantly large volume. The temple has a stone floor, with elegant hardwood timber detailing in the handrails, window frames and soffit, and the walls are washed with a pale amber colouring, which, combined with the timber and soft lighting, create a warm, muted atmosphere.

A dark, floor-lit, underground passageway that follows the same route as the sloped walkway from crematorium building to the temple joins the two buildings. It is here that the coffins can pass from the temple down into the cremation room, and to one of the three furnaces that await.

RITUALS CREMATORIUM
+udeb arquitectos | Guarne, Colombia, 2005

1
A large squat cuboid building, the crematorium rises out of the hillside and is neighboured by a smaller culptural outpost and a series of bridges and paths.

2
Mourners pass from an open square in front of a assed Cor-Ten steel sculpture and through a pathway sliced into the hillside to enter the temple building.

RITUALS CREMATORIUM   **+udeb arquitectos**

3
Marking the first threshold for mourners, a bridge edged in Cor-Ten steel and paved with local stone leads visitors to gather at the entry square, beneath which the crematorium is hidden.

4
Bold T-shaped sections of Cor-Ten steel break up the windowless elevations of the temple, which is clad in local stone. The horizontal bands of Cor-Ten hover above the stone, housing the parapet and admitting light through the space in between.

5
Site plan: A clearly defined pathway at the upper level leads visitors from the car park, across a narrow stream to the sculpture and temple beyond. The lower level allows vehicle access to the crematorium building, which houses the furnace and preparation rooms.

‹ 3   4↑   5↓

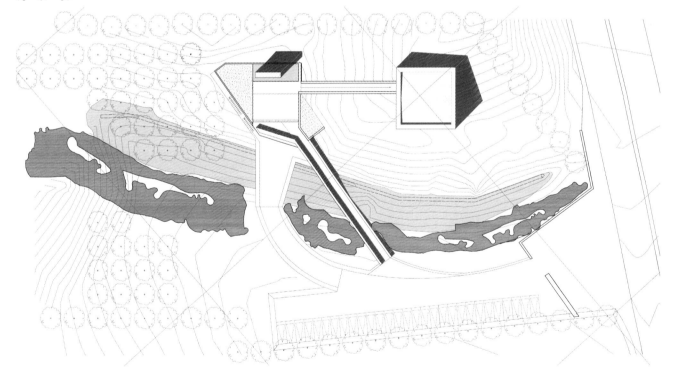

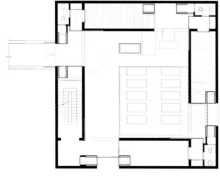

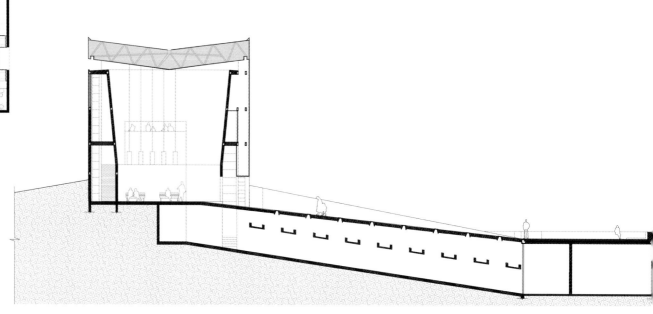

6
Floor plan: The temple is arranged around ten banks of pews oriented towards the lectern and platform on which the deceased body is laid.

7
Section: Public and private spaces of the crematorium complex are clearly delineated. Mourners ascend a defined path and enter the temple, where balcony spaces above can house a choir. The process of cremation occurs discreetly below ground.

8
Roughly square in plan and cuboid in mass, the temple forms an imposing building that offers mouners a reassuring sense of solidity.

9
The small altar of the temple is crafted from hardwood timber, as are the handrails, soffit, window frames and pews.

10
Lights suspended in a grid from the roof help to demarcate seating for the congregation. Hanging two storeys tall, they create intimacy inside what is a significant volume and wash the stone walls with a warm glow.

This monolithic, pared-back church building is on the outskirts of the Schiphol international airport complex, and was built to replace a church that was demolished to make way for the airport extension and the associated development it will bring. The church successfully struck a deal with the developer, Schiphol Real Estate, to help enable the building of the new church. Rotterdam practice Claus van Wageningen Architecten were brought on board to build a new home for a church that belonged to what was, until 2004, known as the Dutch Reform Church, the Dutch branch of Protestantism. In May 2004, after years of dwindling congregations, it merged with the Reformed Churches in the Netherlands and the Evangelical Lutheran Church in the Kingdom of the Netherlands to form the Protestant Church in the Netherlands. This move caused a minor schism within the Dutch Protestant movement, with some more conservative members taking issue with the apparent acceptance of practices such as same-sex marriages and female clergy that the move signified.

This church was designed two years before the change in church structure. Though the church to which it belongs may have become more liberal, from the point of view of some participants, its design is still recognizably Protestant, and a 'low' interpretation at that, with a lack of adornment and luxury that even Luther himself may have been able to countenance. Spatially, the emphasis is on the teaching of the liturgy and of people congregating, rather than on a stage set for giving and receiving the Eucharist that may be more appropriate in a Roman Catholic church. Three large rooms root the organization of the complex: a church, a foyer and a hall for teaching and taking supplementary services. The spiritual hierarchy is articulated in the floor-to-ceiling heights of each space, with the church having the tallest volumes, and the living and service areas the lowest. Around these three spaces are gathered the spaces devoted to the ancillary programmes: the office, kitchen and storage spaces for the church, and the pastor's living space. This residential house, which is located to the left of the main hall, is simple accommodation, with three bedrooms and an open-plan living and kitchen area.

The plan is a rather squat T-shape, or truncated cruciform, with the downward stroke occupied by the rectangular church area, its altar on one of the long walls at the base of the T. Large double doors from the church space open into a rectangular foyer, the heart of the building. The congregation enter from the street into this space from two points: the bottom right of the hall, and the top left, where lobby spaces handle the transition between street and hall.

An orthogonal bell tower positioned to the right of the altar means the church can be seen from the long straight approach of the adjacent road. Unusually, for both programme and context, there is a large rectangular window at head height behind the altar. This window is on the facade facing the road. The car park is tucked away behind the building, and not visible from the street.

From outside, the simple geometric constructions of horizontal and vertical lines fit well within the postwar grid pattern of the Haarlemmermeer polder in which it stands. Yet the sand-coloured concrete, natural stone, generous massing and idiosyncratic street facade mark it out as a special, serious place of worship. The hope is that this resolutely modern church will fit in well with both its current neighbourhood and the one it transforms into, as the area continues to be developed as part of the Schiphol expansion programme.

DUTCH REFORMED CHURCH

Claus van Wageningen Architecten | Rijsenhout, The Netherlands, 2006

1↓   2→

DUTCH REFORMED CHURCH **Claus van Wageningen Architecten**

1
The church's sand-coloured concrete, generous mass, and idiosyncratic street facade demarcate it as a serious place of worship in its context of a gridded, Harlemmermeer polder, near Schiphol airport.

2
An orthogonal bell tower positioned to the right of the altar gives the church visibility from the long, flat approach by road.

3
A simple crucifix on the bell tower, designed by graphic designer Reynoud Homan and sculptor Peter Otto, is the building's only overt religious reference.

4
Simply composed of horizontal and vertical lines, this modern church confers the community's wish to fit with its current neighbourhood and those that are rebuilt as Schiphol is redeveloped.

5, 6
Sections: Spiritual hierarchy is articulated in the different floor-to-ceiling heights. The church (left) has the tallest volume while living and service areas (right) are lowest.

7
Floor plan: The church is composed of three main spaces: a hall (top), foyer (middle) and church (bottom), with ancillary spaces adjacent.

8
The lack of adornment and luxury confer a typically spartan and Protestant interpretation, consistent with its Lutheran origins.

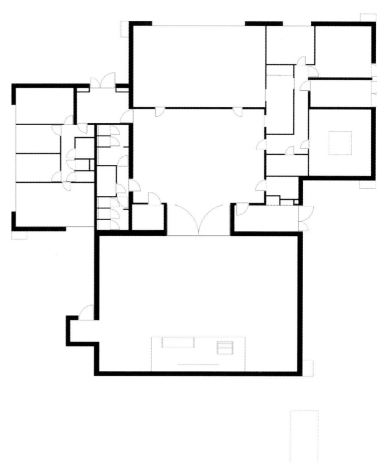

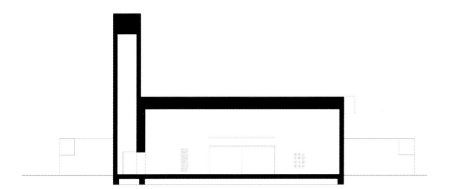

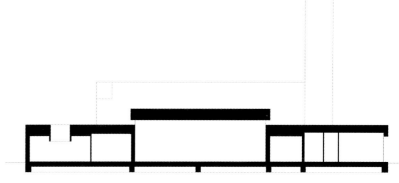

←3   4↓   5↑

6↑   7↗   8↓

9↑ 10↓ 11→

9
Sheltered by the large church volume (left) and lower ancillary spaces, visitors enter the lobby from a large, unmarked car park. The exposed concrete and natural stone are a solemn counterpoint to the primarily agrarian context beyond.

10
The central lobby forms the heart of the complex, acting as a hallway that connects visitors entering from each side of the building. Lined in warm oak panelling and lit with spotlights, its large double doors lead to the church.

11
Consistent with the church's ideology that emphasizes teaching the liturgy rather than an elaborate stage set, the worship space is mostly unadorned. A pre-rusted window screen filters light into the white-washed room that is lit by exposed fluorescent tubes and simple orthogonal furniture.

DUTCH REFORMED CHURCH Claus van Wageningen Architecten

Saint Nicholas of Flue, or Bruder Klaus (Brother Klaus) as he is often affectionately called, is the patron saint of Switzerland, but this chapel dedicated to the extraordinary peasant is in the north of Germany, close to Cologne. Klaus lived in fifteenth-century Switzerland and served as a soldier, a farmer and judge, until a mystical dream warned him of the perils of putting his worldly fulfillment ahead of his spiritual calling, whereupon he decided to leave his wife and ten children to live a life of seclusion and fasting as a hermit. Klaus reportedly existed for nineteen years living on no food other than the Eucharist and was much sought after for his sage advice on matters political, spiritual and moral. As a peasant farmer and ancestral landowner who turned to a life of asceticism, he is a popular saint among agriculturalists and many who work the land profess a close affinity with him.

Enter another much sought-after Swiss character imbued with mystical talents: the carpenter's son and Pritzker Prize-winning architect Peter Zumthor, who works from a small studio a few miles from the small Graubunden town of Chur. Zumthor became involved in the project when he heard that the client, a Roman Catholic farming couple, were to build a chapel dedicated to Brother Klaus, agreeing to design it for a nominal fee – the Swiss architect was working at the time on the widely acclaimed Kolumba Art Museum on the site of a medieval church in nearby Cologne.

The Brother Klaus chapel stands alone in a field in Mechernich, a wine-growing district southwest of the German city. Appropriately, it cuts a lonely figure in the surrounding fields. From the outside it looks like a simple, smooth-faced concrete monolith. It has a peculiar shape: it is an irregular pentagon in plan, with most of its walls chamfered at oblique angles to each other. The chapel rises 12 metres (39 feet) from the ground. The concrete was set by the clients' friends and family using local sand and gravel in twenty-four pours, which can be read in the horizontal banding around the chapel. A triangular steel door, above which a simple cross is notched into the concrete, opens into a very different space to the smooth concrete exterior. Such was his asceticism, Brother Klaus purportedly made a cave his home, and Zumthor's chapel invokes this history.

Inside, a tight corridor of rough, blackened walls opens up to a small chamber which slopes inwards towards a tear-shaped unglazed hole in the roof. This, together with the glass beads embedded in the concrete banding, is the only source of natural light. The floor is made from cast lead. Rain from the openings above gathers in a small basin, sunk into the floor. When this overflows it empties through a simple channel cut into the floor.

The striking interior was created by building a sort of wigwam made from 112 slim tree trunks acting as the concrete formwork. Once the concrete was set, the trees were set alight to burn away, then the charred remains removed, leaving the dramatic effect of the coarse and soot-blackened surfaces. Like Zumthor's celebrated thermal baths at Vals, the mix of rough, sensuous materials creates dramatic and sometimes raw spaces, here used to take the visitor back to the life of a fifteenth-century hermit who chose to give up his prosperous family life in favour of a existence of hunger and exposure to the elements, all for the sake of spiritual clarity.

BROTHER KLAUS FIELD CHAPEL

Peter Zumthor | Mechernich, Germany, 2007

1↓ 2→

1
Dedicated to Saint Nicholas of Flüe, or Bruder Klaus, this chapel in an agrarian setting celebrates the saint and his history as a peasant farmer and ancestral landowner.

2
Standing alone in the middle of a field in Mechernich, the simple, smooth-faced concrete monolith rises 12 metres from the earth and is only accessible by foot, along a gravelled pathway.

BROTHER KLAUS FIELD CHAPEL   **Peter Zumthor**

3↑ 4↓ 5↘ 6→

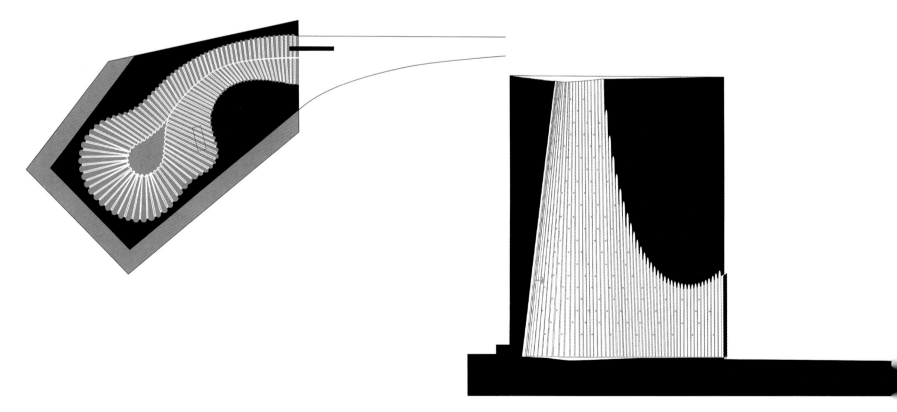

3

Walls of the chapel are chamfered and stand at oblique angles to each other. Formed of concrete mixed from local sand and gravel, the structure was set by the clients' friends and family in twenty-four pours, representing the hours in a day.

4

Floor plan: Shaped as an irregular pentagon, the interior of the chapel is a sort of permanent wigwam forged from 112 slim tree trunks that created the formwork.

5

Section: A tight corridor of rough blackened walls opens up to a small chamber crowned by a tear-shaped hole in the roof. Rain that enters through the opening, collects in a small basin sunk into the floor below.

6

A simple cross notched into the concrete sits above the triangular steel door, which is the point of transition from the smooth exterior to the darkened chapel inside.

7
An unglazed hole in the roof, and hundreds of glass beads embedded in the concrete banding are the only sources of natural light. Modest elements for contemplating Bruder Klaus include a sculpture of him, which is rooted in a floor of cast lead.

8
The dramatic effect of coarse, soot-blackened surfaces was created by setting fire to the formwork of trees once the concrete had set. The compressed, dark interior invokes the purported ascetic cave dwelling of the saint.

←**7**　**8**↑

The LJG Synagogue, built by SeARCH Architects in Amsterdam, was designed for the Liberal Jewish Community of Amsterdam, the largest of the ten Liberal Jewish groups in the Netherlands, and its new synagogue is the second to be constructed in the country since the Holocaust. The building incorporates many classical motifs of Judaism – the menorah, Star of David, and classic numerology – in its formal language, but rearranges them in a manner which suits the contemporary mores of its liberal community. The programme of the building includes synagogue, community centre and offices.

SeARCH recognized an apparent contradiction that they felt was important when it came to designing a synagogue for the community. The synagogue in the Netherlands has not developed a distinct identity of its own as an architectural type. Indeed, one of the themes one can identify is the way in which Dutch synagogues generally downplay the exterior signs of their interior purpose. In contrast to this, the Jewish community itself in the Netherlands is a self-confident one. This dissonance, and the relatively few design stipulations that the Liberal Jewish faith places upon a synagogue, led SeARCH to focus on some basic themes.

In this case it was the positioning of the benches opposite each other, parallel with the axis between Bimah and Ark, and the symbolism of light. This is deployed literally – very large windows flood the synagogue chamber with natural light – and metaphorically: those same windows are shaped in an abstract menorah, one of the enduring symbols of Judaism, that recalls the burning bush discovered by Moses on Mount Sinai.

The synagogue is set within a large rectangular 'box' which faces on to a canal. Ornamental fenestration and patterning on the concrete facades, marking out Stars of David, provides variety to this simple casing. On its short, windowless edge, Hebrew characters are marked out on the facade. The synagogue's most striking feature is the shape of an abstracted menorah cut into its two long elevations. This articulates the central void that cuts through the building, around which the Bimah and the Ark, in which the Torah scrolls are kept, are oriented. Two rows of cantilevered tiers of balcony seating face on to this space, symmetrically arranged across the chamber. At ground level four rows of seating run from window to window on each side. The generous fenestration ensures that the room is filled with light, diffused through panels on the interior of the windows. A rooflight running from the full width allows additional light into the chamber's interior. The light is amplified by the timber used throughout the interior including the benches, lectern, balcony seating and soffit. SeARCH wanted to use symbolism taken from Jewish teaching – light and shade, space and void – in the synagogue. The negative space of the menorah that cuts from the outside inward is the primary move.

Outside the synagogue, the curves of the menorah are expressed in the entrance lobby, and bricks salvaged from the congregation's previous synagogue have been used as a means of connecting the current building with its predecessor. The community spaces fill remaining areas not taken up by the synagogue chamber. In keeping with the importance of numerology in the Jewish faith, special care has been given to the layout of the synagogue chamber. The seven-armed menorah is mirrored by the number of the building's side spaces: four balconies, one central void and a set of benches either side. The synagogue's concrete facade – clad with tiles arranged in a Star of David – has a three-storey leaf-shaped window, repeated on the opposite wall.

LJG SYNAGOGUE

SeARCH | Amsterdam, the Netherlands, 2010

1↓   2→

3 ↑   4 ↓

1
The playful and self-confident community home for the Liberal Jewish Community of Amsterdam is only the second new synagogue to be constructed in the Netherlands since the Holocaust.

2
Set within a large rectangular volume that faces one of the city's canals, the ornamental patterning of the concrete facades marks out Stars of David and creates a distinctive identity for the synagogue.

3
Light is a key symbol used to express Jewish culture in the synagogue. The overscaled windows carry reference to an abstract menorah and also flood the interior chamber with light.

4
The shaped window form appears on both long elevations and is extruded internally to create upper levels of seating and the ceiling of the chamber, all of which are lined in timber.

5
Two rows of symetrically arranged cantilevered seating face the central void the cuts through the building and around which the Bimah and the Ark are oriented.

6
Ground floor plan: Curves of the menorah are expressed in the single-height lobby space, which visitors first encounter.

7
First floor plan: Across all four floors, community areas fill remaining spaces that are not occupied by the central synagogue chamber.

8
Third floor plan: A large central stairwell leads from the lobby to the chamber, in which seating is arranged in four rows that stretch from one window to the other.

9
Section: The importance of numerology in the Jewish faith is referenced in the layout of the chamber, which is mirrored by the adjacent spaces: four balconies, one central void, and benches either side.

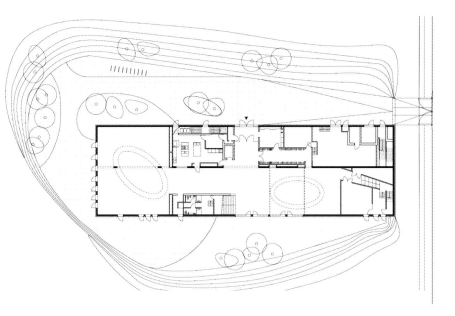

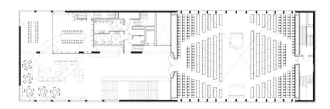

8↑ 9↓

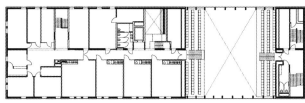

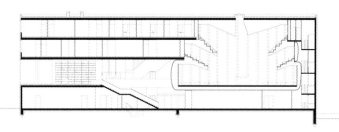

5↓ 6↑ 7↗

10
The threshold to the synagogue is demarcated with brick cladding, which is formed from reclaimed remnants of the previous synagogue as a way to connect the new building with the old.

11
Worshippers ascend a broad flight of stairs from the lobby to reach the first floor and chamber entry. Social areas for conversation and study surround this open-planned level.

12
In contrast to the mostly simple material palette of timber, white walls and pale floors, social areas include colourful rugs and soft furnishings.

10↑ 11↓ 12→

REFLECTION

REFLECTION

For many, religious buildings offer the opportunity to take time out from busy, difficult lives and to snatch a period of calm. This time can be used to pray, to contemplate, to think about the world and one's life: to reflect upon one's position in the world. One of the architects interviewed for this book described the prerequisite for any successful twenty-first-century religious building as being one that 'accomplishes solitude, peace and shelter'. The 'examined life' is a phrase sometimes used in the western world to talk about spiritual and intellectual discovery, and it is something that comes from introspection, from being able to take time for reflection. The way in which religious buildings can help create an environment that encourages reflection are varied; small intimate chapels may be just as successful, in their own ways, as awe-inspiring and monumental cathedrals, a roadside shrine in downtown Tokyo may achieve the same as a large, mountainside Buddhist temple. One of the universal experiences that often brings us – willingly or otherwise – to reflection and introspection is death, the chill blow that intrudes upon our lives and reminds us of our own as well as our loved ones' mortality. Several of the buildings in this chapter deal, obliquely or directly, with death, and create spaces fitting for mourning or preparing for death.

Studio tamassociati's Prayer and Meditation Pavilion (page 142) in a cardiological hospital in Sudan is one of these spaces that deals with the possibility and reality of death. It is a very simple structure, with two separate worshipping spaces, reached via a carefully calibrated transition across a pool of water. The rooms' interiors are non-prescriptive and can be used by adherents of many different faiths. They are spare and straightforward; clean, whitewashed walls are the focus for prayer, solitude, reflection or worship, the materials palette enlivened by the planting of trees within the complex.

Just outside the medieval Italian town of Gubbio, Andrea Dragoni built an extension to the municipality's cemetery that accommodates collective as well as individual reflection (page 154). Visitors walk through the site's narrow 'streets', which echo the town's tight urban fabric, and stop in larger squares, the cemetery's potentially bleak massing and materials palette elevated by artists' installations. When describing this project Dragoni invoked the British Edwardian architect William Richard Lethaby. Lethaby could have been speaking of the importance of spiritual reflection when he said that humans cannot comprehend the world as a whole, but that they must first move away from it, and only after having achieved this detachment can they achieve understanding.

At the Water-Moon Monastery (page 160), at the base of the Datun Mountain in northern Taiwan, Artech have created a building that clearly articulates the values of Zen Buddhism. Its most prominent attribute is a large water feature – a giant Lotus pool in which reflections of the temple facade and the surrounding colonnades play in the rippling water. Plays of light, reflection and shadows are also used to great effect in the main temple. Materials are kept to a limited palette, with polished concrete the primary element of the temple facade and of the cloister. Elsewhere in the complex, teak timber, concrete, glass and limestone are used to create a calm, natural atmosphere appropriate for the contemplation and reflection encouraged by the Buddhist teachings, whether for its full-time residents or for those making a pilgrimage to the monastery.

Bernardo Bader Architekten's Islamic cemetery in Altach (page 148) is among the first state-run Islamic cemeteries in Austria, catering to a community which was long considered to consist merely of temporary visitors to the country but who have settled in the region and become a significant and permanent part of Austrian life. The integration of the religion, not traditionally associated with this region, is reflected well in the *mihrab*, which is made from timber shingles, a popular vernacular building material.

Also in Germany, Bayer & Strobel Architekten won a commission from the state for a new funeral chapel and cemetery in the town of Ingelheim am Rhein (page 166). Bayer & Strobel's response was a neat succession of indoor and outdoor rooms, the largest of which is the chapel, encircled by a heavy retaining wall which presents a bald elevation to the streetscape. The large funeral chapel is marked by a steep gable that protrudes above the front wall, like a triangular peaked hat sitting on the wall. The carefully choreographed procession to the chapel, and relative size of the different rooms and quadrangles within the building, provide many opportunities for both collective and individual reflection.

Mancini Enterprises' Crematorium for G.K.D Charity Trust in Coimbatore (page 174), in the state of Tamil Nadu in south-east India, enabled the local community to hold cremations in as traditional manner as possible; recent, rapid urbanization has made outdoor, riverside pyres less practical. The concrete building offers a sheltered space, yet one open to the breezes that pass through, and is closely integrated with the burial garden in which it sits. Modulated bays make for flexible gathering spaces, allowing room for many or few to gather and pay their final respects in an equally comfortable manner.

How to create a shared religious space that serves a community riven by religious conflict? That was the challenge faced by studio tamassociati for their commission for the Italian NGO, Emergency. Their brief was to produce a prayer and meditation pavilion to serve both Muslim and Christian faiths, as part of a new healthcare complex. Designed to treat patients with heart problems – the only such free facility – for a population of three hundred million, spread over an area of ten million square kilometres (3.8 million square miles).

The centre is in Khartoum, the capital of Sudan, a country that has been beset by internecine conflict for over a decade. Much of this inter-tribal warfare has been separated along religious as well as ethnic lines, with Muslims and Christians regularly coming into conflict. In Sudan, ethnic Arabs make up 39 per cent of the population and Africans 61 per cent. Seventy per cent of Sudanese are Muslims, while the remaining 30 per cent are Christians and members of other religious faiths. Studio tamassociati's approach was to create a chapel that could not only accommodate people from all faiths and ethnic backgrounds, but one that would also foster peaceful coexistence. They

aimed not to overtly privilege any specific religion with their choices concerning internal and external arrangements and decoration, yet sought to build a facility that would meet the functional requirements of the different faiths of visitors to the complex. The centre would also provide spiritual comfort for many who – because of its location as part of a medical complex – may be experiencing traumatic or difficult periods in their lives.

The massing is straightforward. Two large cubes sit adjoining each other, shifted slightly so they are not aligned. A pathway emerges at the point that the two cubes join, bridging the pool over which they sit, while detailing at the buildings' bases makes the cubes appear to hover over the pool. The pool is one of the most visible elements of the design and provides symbolic resonance, yet remains independent of any religion-specific connotations. Bodies of water, conjuring up the idea of oases, are associated with life-giving and health in this part of Africa, located as it is on the fringes of the Sahara Desert. The architects say that the pool also acts as a kind of *cordon sanitaire*; crossing it allows people to leave the clinical world of the hospital complex and enter a more peaceful, spiritual zone.

The two white cubes are separated by a corridor created between the two volumes, and this corridor is partly shaded by a semi-transparent cover of bamboo canes, offering the passage dappled shading. A tree sits within each volume, the architects accentuating the sacredness of these spaces with the planting of an isolated natural object in the otherwise artificial space.

Islam is the dominant faith in Sudan and has more prescriptive rules concerning worship preparation – the need for ablutions prior to prayer and the separation of sexes, for example – and the way in which worship is conducted than does the Christian faith, so the chapel had to subtly cater to these needs. This is done in discreet ways so as not to explicitly render one religion dominant within the architecture. The two separate volumes allow for the separation of men and women while worshipping. The fountains not only help cool the space and create a serene atmosphere but also allow for washing prior to entering the prayer building without being perceived as an overtly Islamic feature. The chapel is a small part of an eight-building medical complex that includes a surgery centre, residential accommodation for visiting relatives and solar panel systems.

PRAYER AND MEDITATION PAVILION
studio tamassociati | Khartoum, Sudan, 2007

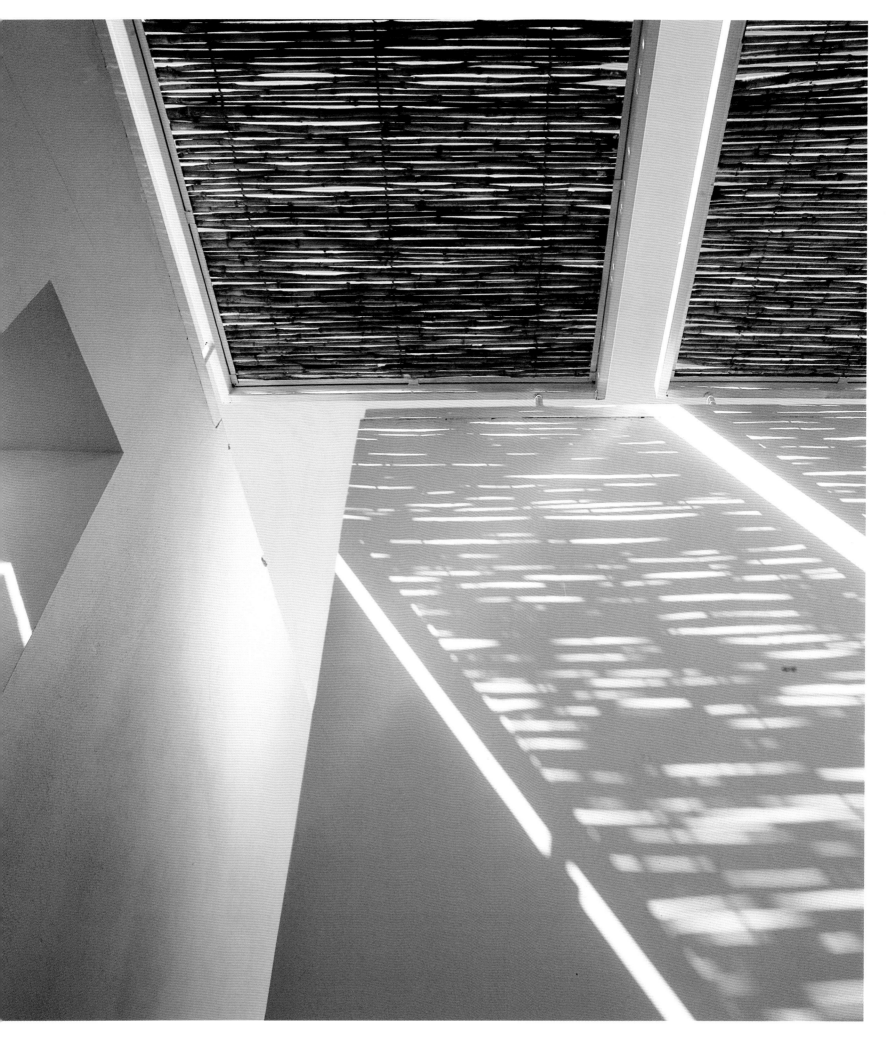

PRAYER AND MEDITATION PAVILION   studio tamassociati

1

The interdenominational worship pavilion in a medical complex is set above a pool of water. In a region for which bodies of water are associated with life and health, it is a highly symbolic aspect of the design.

2

A corridor separates the two volumes and is partly shaded by a semi-transparent cover of bamboo canes, which allows dappled light to enter.

3

Formed of two large cubes that adjoin each other and are slightly misaligned, each of the volumes is accessed from its own pathway, which crosses above the pool.

4

Floor plan: The arrangement of the cubes and material selection subtly accommodates different demands for worship. Islam is the dominant faith in the region and requires preparatory ablutions and the separation of sexes at prayer, which are enabled by the pool of water and separate volumes.

5

Bounded by a low wall and shaded by trees, the two volumes appear to float above a square of shallow water. The pool acts as a *cordon sanitaire*, allowing people to dissociate from the neighbouring clinical hospital environment.

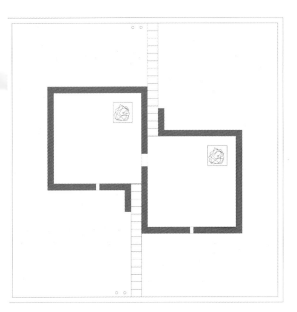

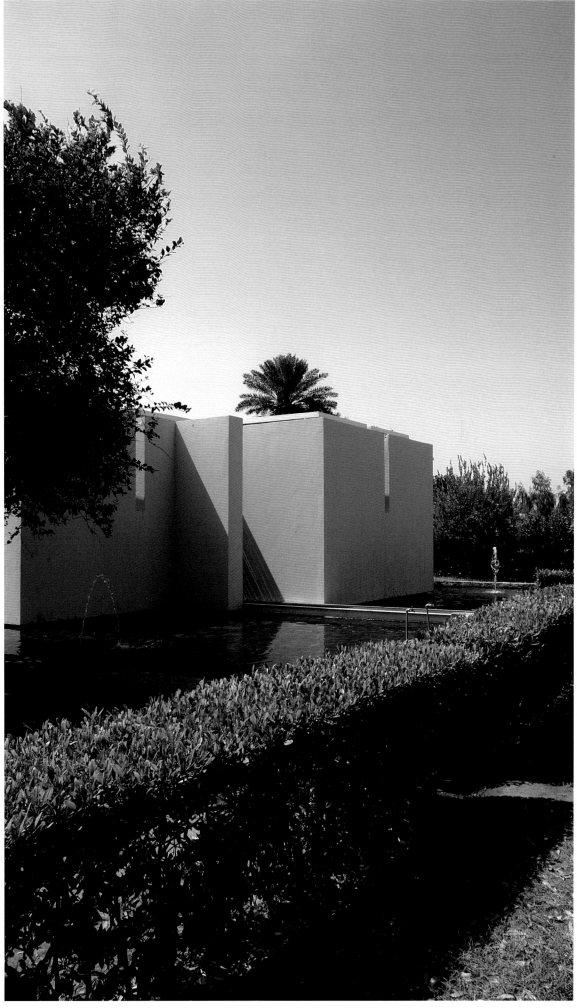

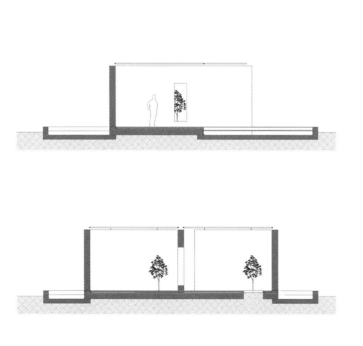

6
The pavilion is a small oasis of calm in the hospital complex that also includes a surgery centre and residential accommodation for visitors.

7
Sections: A single tree sits within each of the two cubes. The use of a natural object in an otherwise man-made space accentuates the pavilion's sacred nature.

8
Designed as an inclusive place to be used by people from all faiths and ethnic backgrounds, the pavilion provides a place for spiritual comfort for those experiencing traumatic periods in their life.

9
This part of Africa, on the fringes of the Sahara Desert, experiences high temperatures and the plain white walls, shading and the evaporative cooling of the pool give respite from the heat.

This Islamic cemetery is the first of its kind in the western Austrian province of Vorarlberg. Indeed, it is of a rare but emergent type that can be seen starting to spring up across Europe: Islamic cemeteries built to contemporary Modernist designs. Over the last fifty years, Austria has seen many immigrants moving to live and work in its cities, often from the south and the east. The 1960s saw an influx of Turkish migrants and most of these people, who were once called *gastarbeiter*, or guest-workers, decided to settle in Austria. This generation of immigrants is now reaching retirement age. The Islamic population of Austria grew during the years of war and unrest in the Balkans following the breakdown of Yugoslavia, while other conflicts brought people from Chechnya, North Africa and Southeast Asia.

The Islamic population of Vorarlberg now makes up approximately 10 per cent of the district, and constitutes the province's second largest religious group, after Roman Catholics. The correct Islamic rites, rituals and means with which the body is prepared and laid to rest differ from Christian burials, so there was a growing need for a facility that would cater for the specific ceremonies and funerary demands of the Muslim community. In 2008 an independent Islamic cemetery was built in Vienna, and the Altach cemetery was intended, partly, to take pressure off the facility in the capital, as well as provide a local resting place for the inhabitants of Vorarlberg.

There are a number of protocols that a Muslim burial must follow. In keeping with the Islamic faith's various prescriptions surrounding cleanliness, the body must undergo a thorough ritual cleansing administered by a specially trained person. Islamic burial protocol requires that the graves face Mecca to ensure that the deceased is ready for prayer on the Day of Resurrection, when Muslims believe that Allah judges all of humanity. With the graves oriented correctly, believers, even in death, are united with the global community of Muslims who prostrate themselves in prayer towards Mecca every day. The cult of the dead familiar to Judaeo-Christian and indexed Confucian cultures is alien to Islam – Muslims are meant to trust in the well-being of the deceased in the afterlife. Consequently their graves have very little ornamentation and they will not have the individual embellishments or mementos which are common in many Christian cemeteries.

In their competition-winning design, local practice Bernardo Bader Architekten proposed a garden that would demarcate the land within the cemetery from the surrounding countryside. The cemetery is broken up into six separate horizontal bays, surrounded by long, low walls, five of which contain the burial fields. In the footprint of the sixth 'finger' is the burial building, with space for taking leave of the deceased, the washing area and a prayer room. Visitors move from the functional areas, through a series of courtyards within this space, to the burial fields beyond. In an interesting symbolic manifestation of the integration of the Islamic inhabitants of this part of Austria, the *mihrab* is made from timber shingles, a popular vernacular building material in Vorarlberg. The carpet of the prayer room was hand-woven in Sarajevo, Bosnia. The low mass of the heavy building is amplified by the horizontal banding where the laid concrete is clearly articulated in the shuttering marks left behind.

In a political environment where the interactions between religious bodies and the states in which they practise has become more contentious, it is worth noting that Altach is a municipal facility, run by the local government for the Muslim community, rather than a facility built and run by the religious group it serves – these social and political mechanics make the Islamic Cemetery the first of its kind in Austria.

ISLAMIC CEMETERY
Bernardo Bader Architekten | Altach, Austria, 2013

3↑ 4↓ 5→

1

This dedicated Islamic cemetery accommodates the differing requirements for correct rites, rituals and preparation of the body for cremation, and the increased demand for these specific ceremonies in Austria and Europe.

2

A large, decorative oak screen extends along the principal elevation and encloses the anteroom.

3

Situated in the Alpine countryside of Vorarlberg, the crematorium is oriented so that the burial fields face Mecca. Even in death, members of the Muslim community are understood to be united with their global community through daily prayers.

4

Imagined as a primal garden, the remains are organized into discrete bays that are demarcated by low red concrete walls that bear the shutter marks of the formwork.

5

Site plan: The complex is arranged in a series of six staggered bays – five contain burial fields, while the crematorium building includes functions for taking leave of the deceased, a washing area and a prayer room.

  Bernardo Bader Architekten

6
Within the burial building, the anteroom provides a transition from the external to the interior: not only in a physical sense, but also spiritually. The screened wall leads down a long corridor to the prayer room.

7
Three metal-mesh curtains hang in front of the whitewashed wooden wall of the prayer room. Gilded wooden shingles woven into the curtains spell the words Allah and Mohammed in Arabic script.

8
Two wooden geometric lattices – one perpendicular, one oblique – intersect and form an overscaled screen that provides shade and decoration to the interior.

9
Unlike Judeo-Christian and Confucian religions, Islamic graves have minimal ornamentation and are not embellished individually.

10
All visitors are greeted and pass by the wooden lattice. Its pattern of the eight-pointed star recalls symbolic Islamic motifs seen in traditional *mashrabiya* screens.

6↑   7↓

←8   9↑   10↓

ISLAMIC CEMETERY **Bernardo Bader Architekten**

On the outskirts of the medieval Italian town of Gubbio lies a cemetery, an arrangement of three concentric square burial plots arranged around a central green. Andrea Dragoni Architetto's addition, a series of fourteen linear blocks punctuated by open squares, or outdoor rooms, is located to the south of the burial areas, reaching the outward edge of the plot. It's intended as an extension to the monumental cemetery, which, by aping the vocabulary of Gubbio's blocks, helps to thread the cemetery back into the imagined fabric of the Umbrian town, becoming in itself a sort of shadow town that mirrors the goings on in the actual town, from which it is separated by a long road. It's an ambitious project that is at times powerful, intimidating and consoling.

In plan there is a series of linear blocks, massive and heavy – being of the earth, or stereotomic to borrow critic Kenneth Frampton's term. These blocks are arranged to form large square enclosures that help to create a rhythm to the sequence and provide space for people to pause and contemplate. The office of Andrea Dragoni was partly inspired by artist James Turrell's Skyspaces – round or square rooms, each with a large oculus in the centre, open to the elements,

which frame a view of the passing skies. The architect describes the way in which these spaces can encourage the mind to wander, to throw off its attachment to the earth and to be able to envisage being part of something bigger; they are spaces in which to focus on the spiritual.

These silent squares are complemented by a series of permanent, site-specific artists' installations that work with the changing effects of light and shadow as the day passes from dawn to dusk – the passing of time, of course, being a central theme in a cemetery. The artworks were designed by Sauro Cardinali and Nicola Renzi, with whom the practice collaborated from the early days of the project.

As well as offering spaces for contemplation, the square indoor rooms provide welcome respite from some of the passageways between the blocks. The narrow runs are, in places, made to feel oppressive by an overhanging volume projecting from the walls at head height. The feeling of compression and discomfort is to some degree reminiscent of some of the spaces created in Peter Eisenman's Holocaust Memorial in Berlin. Using the vocabulary of urban blocks, and the primary and secondary pathways between them,

allows for the use of a range of ceremonial functions, from the monumental to the civic, to the private and intimate. This is one of the great achievements of the project, and it is successful with a minimum of ceremony. Aside from the materials used in some of the installations, the palette is muted: strips of travertine marble are used for both paving – laid horizontally in the pathways to aid the idea of procession, and in the public squares, in concentric squares that direct the view towards the middle of the room – and as the exterior cladding of the blocks. The exterior wall of the cemetery is delineated by the use of red brick.

Describing this project, Andrea Dragoni invokes the words of the British Edwardian architect William Richard Lethaby, who said that human beings cannot understand the world as a whole, but must first move away from it – only after having achieved this detachment can they achieve understanding. In this way the design of the cemetery, with its blocks and squares, is conceived as a model of the world; an order we cannot directly experience, but one which makes perceptible, within the limits of a work of architecture, that which exists on earth.

GUBBIO CEMETERY

Andrea Dragoni Architetto + Francesco Pes | Gubbio, Umbria, Italy, 2011

1↓ 2→

1
A series of towering stone blocks are intended as an extension to the existing monumental cemetery and make reference to the linear urban arrangement of Gubbio, the local Umbrian town.

2
Each of the blocks is separated by a narrow passageway that has a monumental, compressive atmosphere. The daunting scale creates a humbling environment for visitors.

GUBBIO CEMETERY **Andrea Dragoni Architetto + Fransesco Pes**

3
Site plan: Adding to the existing square burial plots arranged around a central green, the fourteen new linear blocks to the lower right of the existing cemetery are also punctuated with contemplative, open spaces.

4
Elevation; Sections: A respite from the repetitive linear blocks is created by four square outdoor rooms that recall James Turrell's Skyspaces, each with a large oculus in the centre.

5
Visitors to the new extension are greeted by a blank roseate concrete elevation that shields the full view of travertine blocks just visible above the datum wall.

‹ 3   4↑   5↓

GUBBIO CEMETERY   **Andrea Dragoni Architetto + Fransesco Pes**

In places, the narrow passages are made more discomforting by overhanging volumes that project from the walls at head height and further compress the space.

A muted material palette of travertine marble is used throughout the project for both paving and as exterior cladding of the blocks.

Contemporary, permanent, site-specific installations by the artists Sauro Cardinali and Nicola Renzi are found at specific points of the project and respond to diurnal change, underlining the effect of passing time.

GUBBIO CEMETERY   Andrea Dragoni Architetto + Fransesco Pes

This large monastery complex was built for the Dharma Drum Mountain Buddhist foundation in the Taiwanese countryside, near Taipei. The name of the monastery came about after initial conversations about the scope of the project with the leader of the Buddhist group. When asked what his vision for the future temple was, Master Sheng Yen, the founder of the monastery and Dharma Drum Buddhist group, answered that he 'saw' the temple in his meditation dhyana. 'It is a flower in space, moon in water', he said. 'Let's name it the Water-Moon Monastery.' And so began the Water-Moon Monastery, whose design combines a powerful, solid presence with the lyrical qualities evoked by its name.

The monastery is built around a large water feature. In keeping with the Buddhist principles of harmony with nature, it was intended to be a building that took full advantage of the surrounding natural beauty and one that strove to provide a tranquil, spiritual place. The monastery makes the most of its rich natural setting: sited on the vast Guandu Plain, it faces the Keelung River and has the Datun Mountain as its backdrop. Light and shade are used to help manipulate the mood and inspire spiritual contemplation within the building. The changing character of nature, the rising and the setting of the sun during the day that changes the shadows throughout the temple, the gentle breeze that plays with the reflections in the giant lotus pond all help create a calm but living building, one that helps remind visitors of the teaching of the Buddha.

Two walls of differing heights provide the boundary lines, as well as a buffer and threshold between the monastery and the neighbouring expressway, which runs alongside the site's boundary. After passing through these walls, and upon entering the temple, visitors are able to view the main hall beyond. In front of this is a large lotus pond, eighty metres (260 feet) in length. The gently rippling reflections of the over-sized colonnades of the temple in the large rectangular pond give the site an ethereal, mesmeric quality. The materials palette is deliberately restrained, with smoothly polished architectural concrete the primary element of the temple facade and of the cloister, with small rectangular alcoves set at regular intervals. Elsewhere in the complex, teak timber, concrete, glass and limestone are used to create a calm, natural atmosphere. Formally the work is kept simple, and together with the pond and the reflections, the aspiration is to convey the spirit of Zen Buddhism.

The interior of the temple is a large, double-height space, capable of accommodating large groups of people. From outside the illusion of a floating timber box is established by panes of glass that run from the ground floor to the first-storey level of the temple, with a timber screen above. This timber screen is carved with characters of the famous text of the Heart Sutra in Chinese script, which casts dappled shadows on to the floor of the large interior of the Grand Hall and on to the altar and statue of Buddha that dominate the most important room of the complex. The theme of evoking spiritual meaning through the use of texts, while providing much-needed screening from the sun, is also used in the corridors throughout the complex: characters of the *Vajracchedika Prajnaparamita Sutra,* or 'Diamond Sutra' which emphasizes the practice of non-attachment, are carved on the prefabricated GRC (glass reinforced concrete) panels. As with the carved characters in the teak screening in the Great Hall, the intention was to imprint the scripture on to the interior surface by sunlight, revealing, in an unspoken manner, the teaching of the Buddha.

WATER-MOON MONASTERY
Kris Yao | Artech | Tapei, Taiwan, 2012

1↓ 2→

3↑   4↓

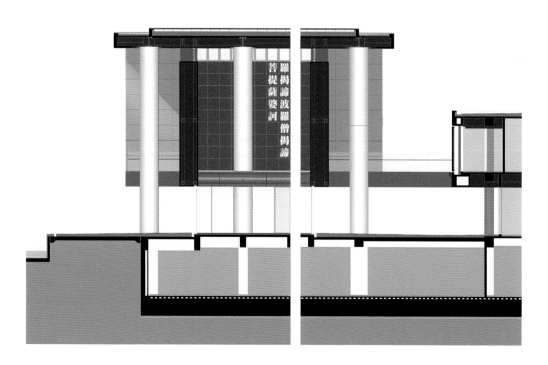

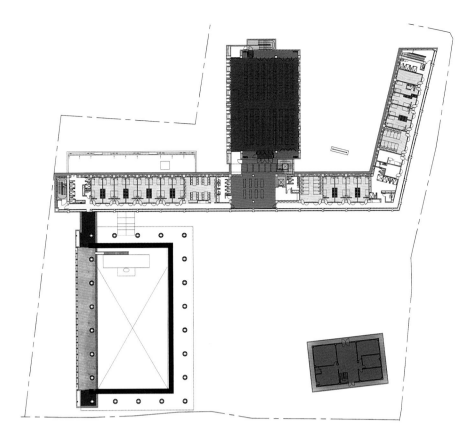

5 ↑   6 ↓

1
Surrounded by the vast Guandu Plain, and the distant Datun Mountains, the monastery is designed in accord with Buddhist principles of harmony with nature.

2
Teachings of the Buddha are inscribed on timber panels, which communicate his teachings in an unspoken way.

3
The expansive lotus pond is a central aspect of the complex. Its appearance changes in response to the rising and setting sun, and wind patterns, reminding visitors of the ephemeral character of nature.

4
Section: The temple is raised one storey above ground level and is arranged as a generous double-height space that can accommodate large groups of people.

5
Plan: The Great Hall of the temple dominates the complex and is accessed from a separate wing that contains cloisters, dining hall and ancillary rooms.

6
In the spirit of Zen Buddhism, the material palette of the monastery is simple and predominated by polished concrete of the temple facade and cloisters.

WATER-MOON MONASTERY   **Kris Yao | Artech Architects**

7
Prefabricated GRC panels in the corridors carry carved characters of the *Vajracchedika Prajnaparamita Sutra*, evoking spiritual meaning and providing necessary screening from the sun.

8
The west walls of the Grand Hall are carved with Chinese characters that narrate the renowned Heart Sutra, illuminating the Hall with sacred text.

9
Dappled shadows from the carved timber walls fall on the teak interior of the Grand Hall – the most important room of the complex, which is dominated by the altar and statues of the Buddha.

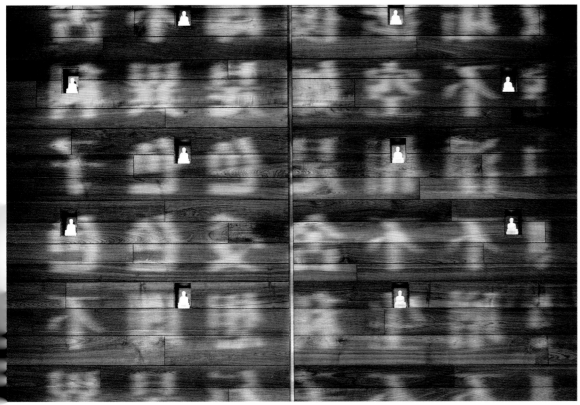

WATER-MOON MONASTERY   **Kris Yao | Artech Architectss**

At this funeral chapel in the German town of Ingelheim am Rhein, Bayer & Strobel Architekten succeeded in creating a building that balances a strong street presence with plenty of indoor and outdoor rooms for solitude, calm and reflection. Each neighbourhood in Ingelheim, a small German town located on the west bank of the Rhine in Rhineland-Palatinate, has its own cemetery. However, the municipality was in need of a larger one, so decided to launch an open competition for the design, which Bayer & Strobel, together with landscape architects JBBUG Landschaftsarchitekten, won. Bayer & Strobel were commissioned by the state client, Stadt Ingelheim am Rhein, to build the complex that would comprise an enclosed cemetery together with chapel and ancillary rooms.

The most striking feature of the completed complex is its pitched-roof funeral hall, which makes it a beacon visible from far around and, from the street elevation, gives it the distinctive look of a pyramid sitting on a platform. The steep gable rises out from a wall built in a yellow stone, taken from quarries nearby, and capped with concrete coping. This wall separates and encloses

the cemetery area from the main street to ensure privacy, establish it as a place of peace and tranquility and to amplify the sense of a threshold that one passes through on entering the complex. The wall also acts as a retaining wall for the more elevated areas of the cemetery that are used for burials. Within this envelope there is a series of intermediary external rooms and a main funeral hall. In front of the complex, between it and the road, are a series of manicured lawns. The complex is entered through a door that sits to the left of the building's main axis.

The drama of the monumental vaulted roof belies the calmness of the series of spaces within. Once inside the building, mourners pass through a space with a small courtyard garden to their left and, once they walk the length of the chapel, pass into a square courtyard area. This section of the complex, designed to help accommodate the congregation before and after the funeral or memorial services, is open to the elements, with shelter provided by a portico which runs round the interior perimeter, like a cloister within a monastery. Three different gradations of stone are used in the courtyard

rooms: the smooth, polished concrete of the flagstones and columns, chipped stone in the decorative gravel beds and the rougher limestone used in the wall. The consistent use of the quarry stone throughout helps give a unity to the complex. In the complex's outdoor rooms, small trees provide pockets of natural flora – three in the large courtyards, one in the smaller – helping to create a calm, peaceful atmosphere, while the path through rooms of varying size helps to create a rhythmic procession to the chapel.

Mourners then pass from the inner courtyard into the foyer of the chapel and then into the chapel itself. The funeral chapel features a double-height space which is top-lit by a rooflight that runs its full length. The architects wanted the funeral hall to exude a sense of hope as well as being a space for mourning, and the finished space lends an almost friendly atmosphere. The gabled roof helps demarcate the importance of the space and gives it a dignified and solemn feel, while staying true to the themes of simplicity and decorative austerity established within the project.

INGELHEIM FUNERAL CHAPEL

Bayer & Strobel Architekten | Ingelheim am Rhein, Germany, 2012

1↓ 2→

INGELHEIM FUNERAL CHAPEL **Bayer & Strobel Architekten**

1
The most striking feature of the cemetery complex is the pyramidal form of the funeral hall that is a highly visible beacon in its low surroundings.

2
The second, more expansive courtyard accommodates the congregation before and after a funeral or memorial service and is open to the elements.

3
A portico runs around the perimeter and shelters the planted courtyard, recalling the cloister of a monastery.

4
Plan: Mourners pass through a carefully planned sequence of rooms that vary in size – from the entry, to the large inner courtyard, the chapel foyer, and then the chapel itself.

5
Long section: A full-length rooflight runs the length of the chapel, flooding the lofty space with natural light. The effect is intended to exude an atmosphere of hope as well as being a place for mourning.

6
Cross section: A double-height space marks the funeral chapel and helps demarcate the importance of the space with a dignified, solemn presence.

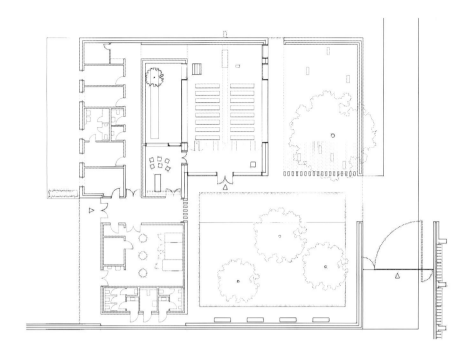

←3 4⌐ 5→ 6⌐

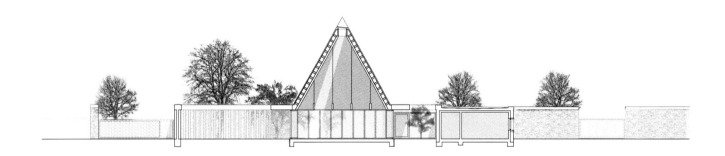

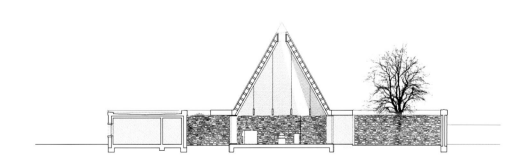

INGELHEIM FUNERAL CHAPEL   **Bayer & Strobel Architekten**

Outdoor rooms in the cemetery complex are planted with small trees and pockets of natural flora that help to create a calm, peaceful atmosphere.

8
Three different gradations of stone are used in the courtyard rooms: smooth, polished concrete of flagstones and columns, chipped stone in the decorative gravel beds, and rougher limestone of walls. The consistent use of quarry stone gives unity to the variety of buildings.

← 7   8 →

9
The drama of the monumental vaulted volume belies the calmness of the space within, which is lined with timber of a similar hue to the stone.

10
A pale material palette is used in the chapel, to imbue peace. The only obvious religious reference is a pared-back cross to the rear wall.

11
Ancillary rooms are arranged in a single block that runs alongside the chapel and accommodate a series of smaller spaces for mourners to meet and gather.

12
A perimeter wall formed of yellowish stone and capped with concrete coping separates and encloses the cemetery from the main street. It ensures privacy and amplifies visitors' sense of passing across a threshold as they enter the complex.

11↑ 12↓

INGELHEIM FUNERAL CHAPEL **Bayer & Strobel Architekten**

The extraordinary pace of urbanization that has taken place across the globe over the last ten years has been felt particularly strongly in India, who has seen its cities grow and expand at incredible rates. Not all civic or religious practices can adapt to keep up with the sudden changes in physical geography, and often populations are left with inadequate or unsatisfactory forms of public activity that are no longer suitable for their much-changed environments. Such was the case in the city of Coimbatore, in the state of Tamil Nadu in Southeast India. Here it was normal practice to cremate bodies on the banks of the river, and for the ceremonies to be attended by large groups of people. Expansion of the city meant that this was no longer practical, hence Mancini Enterprises' brief for a purpose-built crematorium within the heart of a dense urban block.

The intention was to create a humble, straightforward and dignified environment that evoked the traditional location and practices of cremation, while at the same time providing suitable facilities. The complex sits within a walled garden, and is composed of two separate pavilion buildings together with courtyards, an administrative building and smaller pavilion buildings in which ashes and urns are interred. All of the areas are exposed to the air, helping to maintain the informality and connection to customary outdoor, riverside cremations, while also allowing for flexibility when it comes to numbers of mourners – the pavilions can be an intimate home to a small gathering, or equally an expansive space out of which hundreds of mourners can spill, depending on the size of the ceremony.

All parts of the pavilions are concrete, with the exceptions of a rendered outside wall that faces the street, and the drainage chains. The last rites are performed in these pavilion spaces where the mourners gather before the body is taken into the furnace area. The next morning family members collect the ashes from the administration building and proceed into the garden where smaller pavilions give shelter to the required rituals for the final goodbye to departed friends or relatives. The austere materials palette of the main pavilions is softened and contrasted by the lush vegetation of the gardens in which they sit.

The crematorium's buildings are located down a narrow passage that opens up into a small courtyard area in front of the main entrance to the two pavilions. On the approach to the pavilions, mourners can gather outside and, if necessary in inclement weather, under the overhang of the concrete soffit of the pavilions, which project several metres from the whitewashed wall that marks the threshold of the crematorium. The pavilion's roof is supported by four bays of four concrete columns. In between each bay is a section of whitewashed wall, apart from at the entrance point, where the congregation passes through a gap in the bays into the pavilion. Once inside the pavilion there are two rooms, each with a large concrete slab at knee height, in the middle of the indoor room, where the deceased is laid. Passing through the pavilion they encounter the garden area, an oasis of natural vegetation after the utilitarian harshness of the all-concrete interiors of the buildings. As well as long grasses and small, manicured shrubs, the garden is planted with mature trees that help reinforce the feeling of a small sanctuary. The sanctuary is very much of nature, but one with an intimacy and privacy that helps it accommodate the gathering of people marking the passing of their loved ones.

CREMATORIUM FOR GKD CHARITY TRUST
Mancini Enterprises | Coimbatore, Tamil Nadu, India, 2013

1↓ 2→

3↑ 4↓

1

In the heart of a dense urban block of central Coimbatore, Southeast India, the crematorium is a new and necessary addition to cope with rapidly increasing civic demands.

2

All parts of the pavilion are made of concrete, to establish an atmosphere that is both monumental and utilitarian.

3

A natural oasis, the garden is a soft contrast to the utilitarian harshness of the concrete interiors. Its planting of long grasses, manicured shrubs and mature trees reinforce its role as a small sanctuary.

4

Mourners can gather outside of, and shelter underneath, the overhanging concrete soffit of each pavilion, which project several metres beyond the whitewashed walls.

5

Site plan: Located within a walled garden, the complex is composed of two separate pavilion buildings together with courtyards, an administrative building and smaller pavilions in which ashes and urns are interred.

6

Cross section: Last rites are performed in the large pavilion spaces where mourners gather before the body is taken to the furnace.

7

Cross section: Following cremation, family members collect ashes from the administration building at the entrance to the complex and carry the remains to smaller columbarium pavilions in the gardens.

5↑ 6↓ 7↘

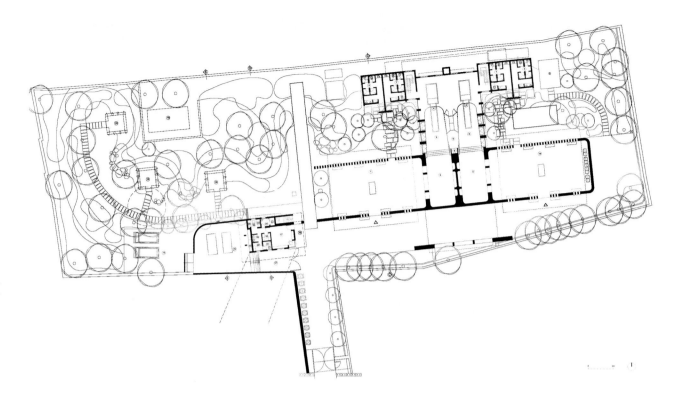

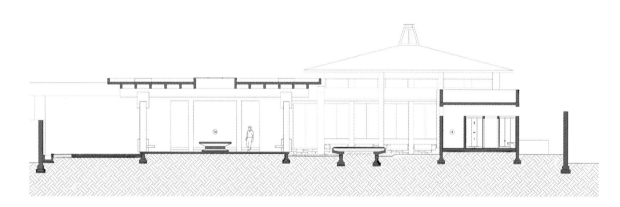

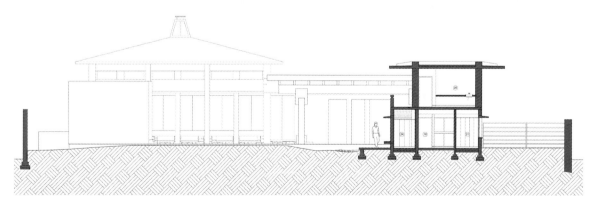

CREMATORIUM FOR GKD CHARITY TRUST **Mancini Enterprises**

8
Each of the pavilion roofs is supported by a series of four robust concrete columns that create four bays. Demarcated by sections of whitewashed walls, the congregation passes through a gap in the bay to enter each pavilion.

9
Rain is channelled from the roof via lengths of chain suspended from projecting beams. This detail is one of the few exceptions to the predominant concrete palette.

10
A large concrete slab at knee height, where the body is laid, is the focus of each pavilion. Rooms are deliberately open to the elements, in an effort to connect with traditional Indian riverside cremations and to allow room for either an intimate ceremony or for hundreds of mourners to spill out of.

REVELATION

REVELATION

Revelation is a concept that permeates many religious cultures. The idea of a set of truths or wisdom being suddenly or gradually revealed to an individual or group of people is present in the Abrahamic faiths and in Buddhist thought. Throughout the Old Testament there are many instances of revelation that remain important to the Jewish faith, from the dreams of Joseph, the warnings that saw God's angel 'pass over' the Jewish people, to Moses's many meetings with angels bearing God's message. The New Testament contains many dramatic examples of revelation, where individuals are struck by a sudden metanoia – or a change of heart – and often become enthusiastic evangelists as a result. One thinks in particular of Saul's revelation ('scales fell from his eyes') on the road to Damascus, which led to his conversion, his taking on the name of Paul, and his later beatification as Saint Paul. The foundation of the Islamic faith, the five pillars of Islam, the Koran, and the Hadiths, which outline correct daily protocol, are all a result of Mohammed's divine revelations, which he recorded to form the basis of these sacred texts.

Within architecture, Le Corbusier, a man keenly aware of the importance of the metaphysical, used the analogy of 'ineffable space': a spine-tingling state, impossible to describe, but which must be felt, that could suddenly arise through the successful and harmonious coalescence of built elements.

The buildings in this chapter all aim, in their own way, to facilitate personal and communal revelation. Many religious groups advocate personal pilgrimage, whether it be Muslims to Mecca or Hindus to their holy temples. Given the importance given by many faiths to the idea of the retreat or pilgrimage – that of exposing oneself to hardship and of deliberately cutting oneself away from the consolations of society – as a means of achieving revelation, it is appropriate that three of these projects are shelters on pilgrimage routes.

Luis Aldrete's Pilgrim Route Shelters (page 202) are two of a series designed by different architects throughout the Sierra Madre Occidental mountain range of Jalisco in Mexico, the location of a pilgrimage dedicated to the adoration to the Virgin of Talpa. Here the rooms are kept very simple, designed solely to provide shelter and a degree of comfort for the passing traveller. The simple brick construction is punctured, allowing light and breeze to permeate, without overly exposing the shelters' interiors.

Undurraga Devés Arquitectos Auco Chapel in Los Andes, Chile (page 208) stands out from the surrounding terrain, helped by a large elevated cross in the parking lot and the distinctiveness of its exterior. The building appears to have completely blank facades – no door or windows are visible anywhere – and has fins projecting from each of its four walls. Only by approaching the chapel can one see that the building's entrance takes the visitor into the belly of the earth, down a ramp going beneath ground, where the congregation sits, with the building's superstructure sitting above it – a perfect combination of Semper's stereotomic and tectonic architecture.

In the hills above Acapulco, Mexico, BNKR Arquitectura built the Sunset Chapel (page 184), a memorial chapel whose distinctive chamfering and boulder-like massing echo the landscape in which it sits. The chapel was designed in a sensitive way to conserve and make the most of the dramatic views from its second-storey gathering space.

The other types of building in this chapter could be contrasted with the single-room shelter or chapel, in that they are complexes built for a permanent community, with a complex set of differing and combined programmes. Randić-Turato's Pope John Paul II Hall (page 190) was built for the Franciscan order who occupy a place of Marian pilgrimage above the Adriatic coast and the Croatian port town of Rijeka. The hall creates a new square and offers plenty of space to accommodate pilgrims to The Shrine of Our Lady of Trsat, which is very busy on feast days. This space was designed to accommodate congregating pilgrims spilling out of the monastery, as well as to host large outdoor services. The sheltered colonnade creates impromptu niches for people to escape the sun after the long journey.

Chushin-ji Temple Priest's Quarters by Katsuhiro Miyamoto & Associates (page 196) occupies a spot in the Japanese mountains that has been in use by Buddhist monks for over 550 years. The thick, sweeping concrete roof is designed to last 200 years, while the timber interior dwelling spaces are designed to a more loose-fit specification, and can be easily modified according to the head priest's changing needs.

In Jyväskylä, Finland, Office for Peripheral Architecture's Kuokkala Church (page 214) has created a new landmark for the area, and established a strong civic presence on the square. The church has a distinctive, chamfered mass to it, which neatly encloses the several function rooms within. The spectacular timber-lined nave and central worship space combine traditional hand-made techniques together with contemporary machine-produced laminated members.

Perched within a copse in the hills above Acapulco on the Pacific coast of Mexico there appears to be a boulder, larger than the other granite rocks that surround it, that teeters on the brink, ready to roll down the hillside to the Mexican holiday resort below. Closer inspection reveals the horizontal banding of poured concrete, and that what at first seemed to be a large crack in the boulder is in fact a doorway. Passing through the triangular aperture takes visitors into an austere faceted concrete lobby, from which they climb a staircase to reach a chapel above. The Sunset Chapel was designed as a place to mark the passing of loved ones: beneath and around the chapel, and part of the architect's brief, was the inclusion of rows of burial crypts. BNKR Arquitectura's first religious commission was for a wedding chapel. This, their second, marks the other end of people's life journeys.

The peculiar, faceted geometries of the Sunset Chapel are derived from the architects consciously mimicking the boulders in the surrounding landscape, but more prosaic factors also shaped the formal language of the chapel. The architects were instructed to make the most of the site's stunning views and the brief specified that the sun must set exactly behind the altar cross set into the glazed west wall. A copse of trees and a huge boulder obstructed the principal views, but felling the trees and demolishing the boulder would not have been countenanced for reasons environmental, spiritual, ethical – and not least economical. Raising the chapel above them, however, could.

Lifting the chapel above the line of the trees made uninterrupted views possible. A large picture window makes the most of this, and frames the altar cross, and twice a year, on both equinoxes, the sun sets exactly behind it. The architects were keen to minimize the effect the building had on the surrounding plant life, which includes rare and exotic flora, so reduced its footprint to half that of the floor area on its upper level, a move which amplified the boulder-like characteristics of the building.

The pews of the upper-floor chapel are set in concrete. Throughout the interior, detailing is spare. The only deviation from the chapel's concrete palette is the glazed balustrade along the perimeter of the upper floor and the steel rods from which the staircase treads hang.

Viewed from outside, the altar cross becomes a beacon for mourners or passersby walking through the scrub. The tension created by the contrast between the solidity of the concrete with the apparent precariousness of the building's form and position – seemingly just one push from toppling down the hill – reflects the sometimes ambivalent requirements we have for religious buildings that host the rituals we use to commemorate the death of friends and family. This is such a building, one that is at once intimate and awe-inspiring, capable of transcending individuals, but also one that is sensitive to commemorating them. As well as offering a pleasing metaphor for the fragility of life – that something so robust can appear unstable – for Christian mourners the image of a boulder can be a symbol of hope: reminding mourners of the boulder that sealed Jesus Christ's tomb, and which, when it was found rolled away, was a sign of his resurrection and the hope that religion can bring despite the presence of death.

SUNSET CHAPEL
BNKR Arquitectura | Acapulco, Guerrero, Mexico, 2011

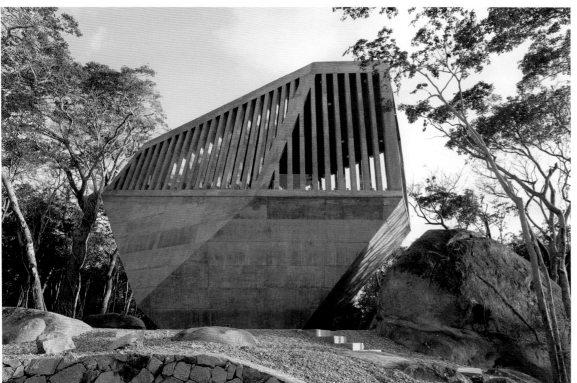

1
Marked by horizontal bands of concrete, the chapel appears as a large boulder and is reached via a simple stone staircase. Its doorway appears to be little more than a great crack in the rock.

2
The chapel is orientated so that the sun sets exactly behind the altar cross in the west-facing wall twice a year during the spring and autumn equinoxes.

3
Large trees and a gigantic boulder threatened to block the sunset view. In order to accommodate these obstructions in an ethical, spiritual, environmental and economical way, the chapel was raised up five metres.

4
To minimize impact on the rare exotic flora nearby, the building footprint is half the size of the upper level floor area, amplifying its boulder-like appearance.

5
Site plan: The peculiar, faceted geometry of the Sunset Chapel is derived from the architect's conscious mimicry of boulders in the surrounding landscape.

6
Ground floor plan: From the narrow entry, mourners ascend a spiralling staircase of concrete, its treads suspended from narrow steel rods.

7
First floor plan: Fourteen concrete pews are snugly arranged in the irregular hexagonal floorplate, which is also formed of cast concrete.

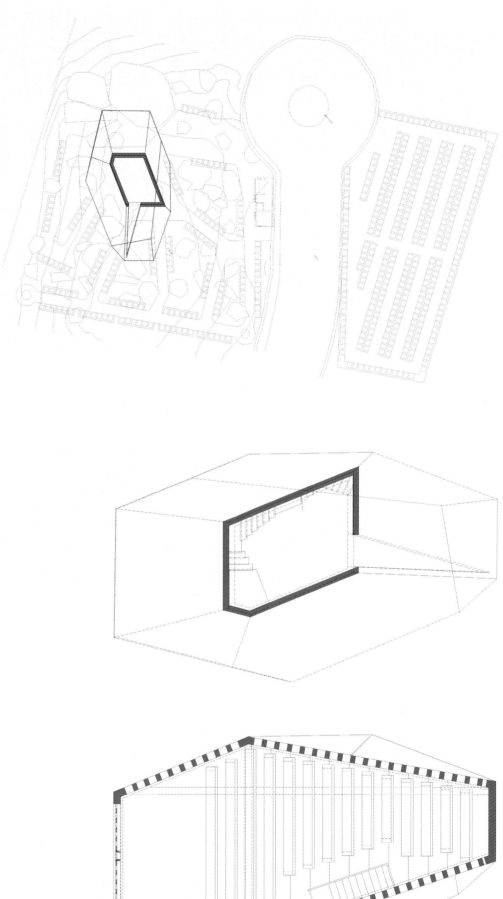

5↑ 6→ 7↓

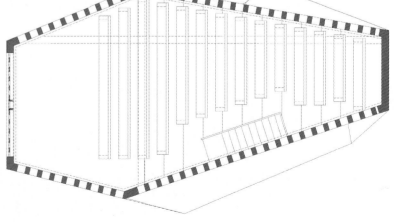

8

Viewed from afar, the altar cross is a beacon that helps mourners or visitors locate the camouflaged object in its scrubland setting.

9

Narrow slices of glazing held within the chapel's concrete ribs admit light and allow sweeping views across the landscape and to the waters of Acapulco below.

10

Though intimate, this building is also awe-inspiring. It is a place that is capable of transcending individuals but is also sensitive to commemorating them.

11

The Sunset Chapel is a place to mark the passing of loved ones: rows of crypts are located beneath the chapel. BNKR Arquitectura's first religious commission was for a wedding chapel. This, their second, marks the other end of the human life journey.

10↑ 11↓

High above the Adriatic coastline, in the port city of Rijeka, is The Shrine of Our Lady of Trsat. This Roman Catholic place of devotion marks the mysterious happening in May 1291, when fragments of the house of Mary, mother of Jesus Christ, supposedly dislodged themselves from their Nazareth resting place and miraculously appeared on the hilltop of Trsat, a district of Rijeka, in what is now Croatia. Years later they were said to have disappeared, as quickly as they had arrived, to be found later in the Italian town of Loreto. Though the stay of the holy fragments was short, the incident was sufficient to turn Trsat into a popular place of pilgrimage. In the fifteenth century Franciscan friars, the site's appointed guardians, built a monastery, school and hospital alongside the shrine. Today it remains an important destination for Marian devotion.

The shrine's annual highpoint is the Feast of the Assumption in August, when Catholics celebrate Mary's death and entry into heaven, and thousands of pilgrims stream into the town and climb the 561 steps, built by Croatian warlord Petar Kružić in 1531, from the Rijeka waterfront to the monastery. More recently it became clear that the monastery needed to increase the capacity of its buildings to tend to the practical and spiritual needs of this annual influx of visitors, in keeping with the Franciscan order's reputation for hospitality. The answer was this new complex, designed by the local architect Randić Turato.

They removed old service buildings at the boundary of the monastery and pushed back the site's eastern wall to make way for a new entrance and a public pathway that follows the site's perimeter. The new buildings consist of a three-storey hall, cloister and courtyards, which sit adjacent to the existing monastery. The centrepiece hall – a large, hipped barn built in terracotta brick – is surrounded by an L-shaped colonnade-cum-cloister that frames two edges of a large new square. This space is designed to accommodate congregating pilgrims spilling out from the monastery, as well as to house large outdoor religious services. The people this public space hosts bring the square, which sits between the old and the new, to life. Concrete fins set at irregular intervals along the colonnade of the cloister create impromptu niches for people to gather, whether to escape the sun, or to have their confession heard on a busy feast day. Within, the cloister space hosts a variety of exhibitions on its shaded interior walls.

The theme of a series of porous spaces set up by the square and porticos is picked up in the red brick facade and roof of the terracotta hall, where the bricks have been spaced to allow light to permeate the hall, and create a pattern akin to a loosely woven fabric. The hall itself is used for both secular and religious gatherings, hence its sparsely decorated interior. A strip of papal gold runs horizontally behind the altar and a yellow band runs vertically from wall to ceiling, following the line of the window next to it – the rest of the timber-lined interior is white. As well as the choir space, which overlooks the main hall, the hall has several ancillary functions within its envelope: an office, library, café and gallery. John Paul II, the Polish-born pope who both lived under, and was a strong critic of, communism, visited the site in 2003 and prayed at The Shrine of Our Lady of Trsat. John Paul II gave his blessing to the friar's expansion plans and the hall later took his name.

POPE JOHN PAUL II HALL
Randić Turato | Rijeka, Croatia, 2008

1↓ 2→

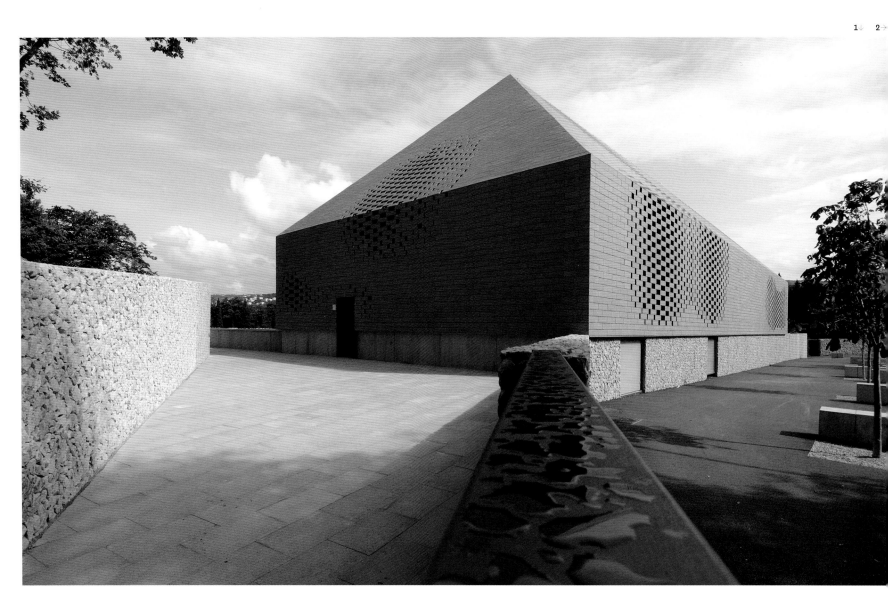

1
In keeping with the Franciscan order's emphasis on hospitality, a large new barn-like terracotta hall is part of the monastery's expansion to accommodate thousands of annual visitors to this pilgrimage site.

2
Gaps in the brick cladding help to moderate the expanse of the building, bringing light and fresh air into the hall interior.

POPE JOHN PAUL II HALL   **Randić Turato**

3↑ 4↓ 5↘

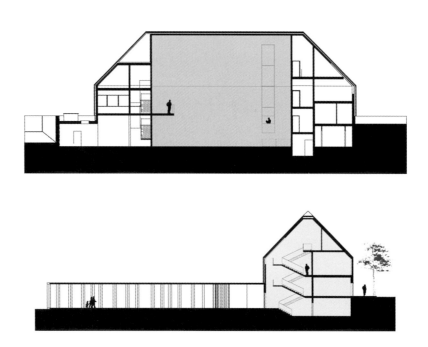

3
A storey-height stone wall provides a datum out of which the hall's terracotta brick envelope rises. It also provides a robust buffer for street and traffic noise.

4
Cross-section: The main square, hall and cloisters are all set below street level for increased privacy.

5
Long section: A triple-height hall for worship is the central focus of the new extension while ancillary functions of the monastery are located at its perimeter.

6
Standing between the existing retained facilities and the new buildings, the square can hold pilgrims spilling from the hall and accommodate large outdoor services.

7
The large hip-roofed building is surrounded by an L-shaped colonnade that acts as a cloister and frames the edges of a new public square, as well as providing sun shelter.

6↑ 7↓

POPE JOHN PAUL II HALL **Randić Turato**

8↑ 9↓

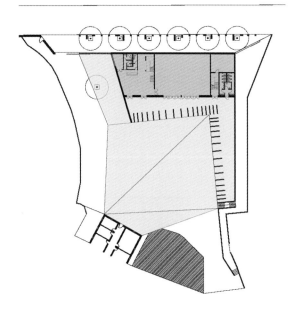

8
A view from the choir, which is elevated one storey above the congregation. The interior is timber-lined and illuminated with long, suspended pendant lights that create a more intimate feel in the lofty volume.

9
Floor plan: The main hall is flanked by a deep colonnade, formed of concrete fins set at irregular intervals along its length. These create impromptu niches for people to gather, to make a confession on busy days, or to host exhibitions.

10
Exploded isometric: The monastery is composed of three main elements – a large terracotta skin, timber-lined hall, and the single-height cloisters.

11
A sash of papal gold borders the strip windows within the hall. Its glistening presence enlivens an otherwise sober interior, which is used for both secular and religious occasions.

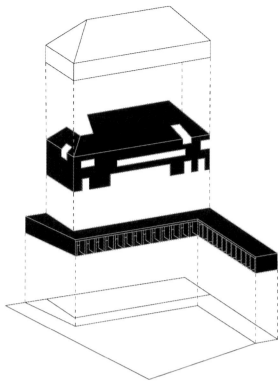

10↑ 11↓

POPE JOHN PAUL II HALL   **Randić Turato**

Katsuhiro Miyamoto & Associates have created a contemporary reworking of one of the key design features of traditional Zen Buddhist temples – the roof with upturned corners – in its design for a high priest's dwelling place, developing an architecture that has its roots in the past yet has a modern, relevant sensibility. The large sweeping roof that is this building's main gesture is made from concrete, and instead of the usual timber supports, is held up by three concrete columns. This sweeping roof provides protection for the timber structure beneath, while its exuberant form establishes it as a publicly accessible building and one of the most important structures in this small complex nestled in the Japanese Alps, close to the town of Minowa, in the Nagano Prefecture on the island of Honshu.

The monastery has hosted Buddhist worship for almost six centuries and the current head priest is the thirty-first successor to the founding monk. Katsuhiro Miyamoto & Associates were called upon to build the *Kuri*, or priest's quarters. *Kuri* are traditionally the places within temple complexes where food is prepared for the head priest and his family and guests, and are adjacent to the main hall and the reception hall. But recently the programme of *Kuri* have changed, to encompass certain administration and ceremonial needs as well as the more usual food preparation requirements. Here, at Chushin-ji, the head priest wanted to ensure that there was appropriate accommodation for himself and his family, but also to have provision to open up the rooms, hosting events like exhibitions, concerts and lectures, for locals to enjoy.

The unusual roof is designed to offer a symbol of unchanging robustness and of eternity – it is built to withstand the heavy snowfall and earthquakes that the area is prone to. The structure beneath, which hosts the interior programme of the monastery, is not affixed to the roof, and can be altered according to the changing needs of the monastery. The architects came to settle on this approach after having observed that many of the existing quarters had been adapted, repaired or altered over the years but that the roofs were largely untouched. Hence the decision to build a roof that would last 100 to 200 years. The concrete's high thermal mass helps keep the temperature constant, cooling the buildings in summer and keeping them warm in winter. The tension between the timelessness and transience integral to Buddhism is thus literally articulated in the architecture while providing a useful adaptability – both a pragmatic and poetic resolution.

Inside, the timber structure, Japanese carpentry, paper walls and timber flooring offers a warm counterpoint to the cool concrete. The nested timber structure hosts the residential and communal areas. The first floor has an office and a large living room with an adjacent porch intended to function as the communal space, with an earthen floor. Upstairs on the second floor is the private residential area with four bedrooms and interconnected living areas. At the highest point above the apex of the concrete roof is a small loft space. As in traditional Japanese housing, sunlight comes in through the sides of the building, diffused through windows and paper wall panels, and is reflected by the white soffit of the concrete roof and the highly reflective polished timber flooring. A covered walkway links the new building with the existing temple complex and the overhang of the roof provides a small, sheltered outdoor area under which visitors can congregate or sit.

CHUSHIN-JI TEMPLE PRIEST'S QUARTERS

Katsuhiro Miyamoto & Associates | Honshu, Nagano, Japan, 2009

CHUSHIN-JI TEMPLE PRIEST'S QUARTERS Katsuhiro Miyamoto & Associates

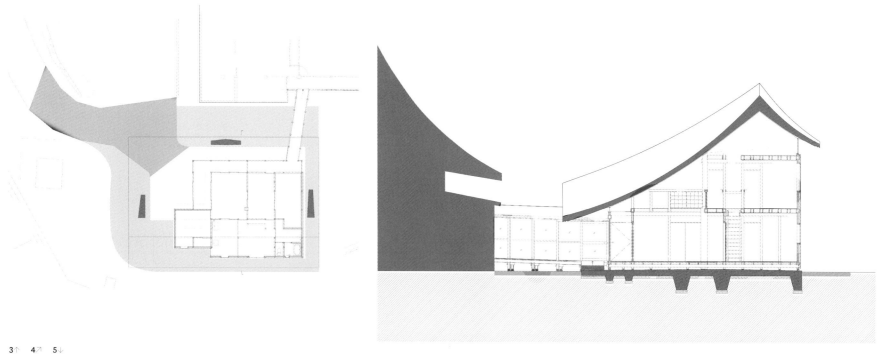

3↑ 4↗ 5↓

1

Prominent upturned corners of this pavilion mark it out as one of the most important structures in this small complex, nestled in the Japanese Alps, close to Minowa.

2

The concrete roof and pillars are designed as permanent fixtures while the timber rooms nested beneath can be removed or adapted over time.

3

Floor plan: In distinction from traditional *Kuri*, this hall ensures appropriate accommodation for the head priest and can be used to host events for public enjoyment, such as exhibitions, concerts and lectures.

4

Section: The *Kuri* stands adjacent to the main hall of the monastery, which has hosted Buddhist worship for almost six centuries.

5

Though unusual, the roof is intended to offer visitors a symbol of eternity and robustness. It also offers a practical function, to withstand the heavy snow and earthquakes that this region experiences regularly.

6

Concrete has a high thermal mass which aids the steady internal temperature of the *Kuri* during hot summers and freezing winter months.

7

A wooden structure enclosing the building hosts interior functions and is not affixed to the roof, offering an apposite interpretation of tension between endurance and transience that is integral to Buddhist philosophy.

6 ↑   7 ↓

　CHUSHIN-JI TEMPLE PRIEST'S QUARTERS　**Katsuhiro Miyamoto & Associates**

8
Organized as one large space that is simply divided by timber framing and paper walls, the central communal space is the focus of the new building.

9
A small loft space is tucked beneath the apex of the concrete roof. The level below houses the four bedrooms and interconnected living areas for the priest and his family.

10
Similar to a traditional Japanese building, sunlight enters through the sides of the building. It is diffused by windows and paper walls and reflects off the white concrete soffit and highly polished timber floors.

11
An external porch with a large earthen floor is protected by the overhanging eaves and forms an extension to the main living space.

8↑ 9↓

10↑ 11↓

The tradition of the pilgrimage, the journey that both helps prove and develop one's spirituality, and of welcoming travelling pilgrims with modest accommodation and provisions, goes back many thousands of years. The tradition of the travelling holy man and, indeed, whole tribes, is evident in the stories of Moses in the Old Testament and can also be seen in the New Testament. In the Islamic faith, the obligation to make the Hajj, the pilgrimage to Mecca, at least once in one's lifetime, is one of the five pillars of Islam and, before the age of jumbo jets and air-conditioning, many Muslims would spend part of their lifetime journeying across North Africa and the Middle East to reach Mecca. Similarly, pilgrimage to the holy land became popular in the medieval era for Christians and in the last few centuries many other places of pilgrimage have been established – Lourdes in France, Medjugorje in Bosnia and Herzegovina – alongside more time-honoured holy sites like Santiago de Compostela in northern Spain.

The Pilgrim Route Shelters are a pair of refuges for pilgrims making the 117 kilometre (72 mile) pilgrimage, dedicated to the adoration of the Virgin of Talpa, through the Sierra Madre Occidental mountain range of Jalisco in Mexico. Luis Aldrete designed a modular system that could be used across both shelters, and which would allow them to be adapted and grow in the future, if required. The two materials used in the construction of the shelters are a type of adobe brick and a clay lintel. The structures are steel-framed, with concrete roofs and paving. Both shelters are long and narrow affairs, with a long room abutted by an ablutions block, and they both sit on hillsides, at right angles to the direction of the slope.

The first refuge, the Albergue Atenguillo pilgrim shelter has a simple, rectangular plan. At the end closest to the entrance is the toilet block. This is enclosed from the rest of the shelter, which is made up of one large volume, in effect broken into a sequence of three smaller rooms by partitions that project across the room. The second refuge, the Albergue Estanzuela, has a slightly more sophisticated plan. The rectangular rooms are slightly chamfered here, the long structure made up of the ablutions block and against this, two elongated pentagons sitting end to end, kinking round the hillside. The structure tapers towards its end and, unlike the Albergue Anteguillo, has a large paved living space outside the shelter.

The diffusion of light is a theme that both of the shelters share, referencing the dappled light cast by shadows of oak leaves from the trees which line the pilgrimage route. The simple brick construction allows for gaps in the bond to be left at regular intervals, which helps bring light into the structures while mitigating against harsh illumination at the height of the day. Luis Aldrete decided against sophisticated glazing, which would be costly and, perhaps more importantly, sever the link between the countryside outside and the interior of the shelter. In both shelters unbroken bonds of bricks scale the height of the door lintel, with the broken bond used at the second storey level to bring light into the building. The latticework also allows a breeze to blow through the structure and refresh the interior space. Both shelters use adobe bricks made from soil gathered at the site, helping them blend into the landscape. These two buildings are part of a series of commissions of high-profile architects and artists who have created shelters for the route, including Ai Weiwei (Fake Design), Tatiana Bilbao, Christ & Gantenbein, Dellekamp Arquitectos, Alejandro Aravena (Elemental), Godoylab, HHF Architects, and Rozana Montiel (Periférica).

PILGRIM ROUTE SHELTERS

Luis Aldrete | Jalisco, Mexico, 2010

1↓   2→

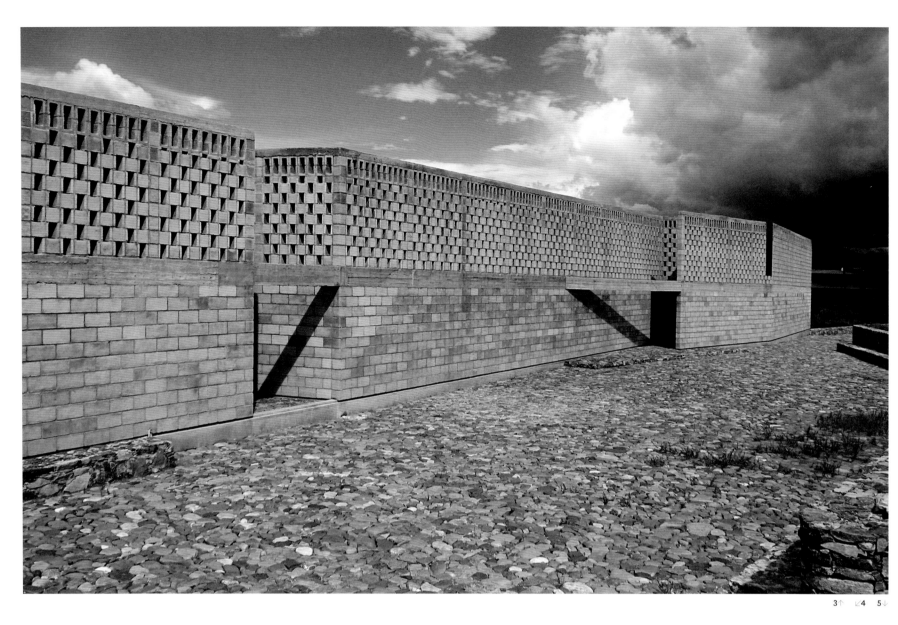

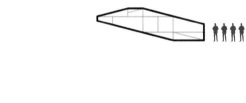

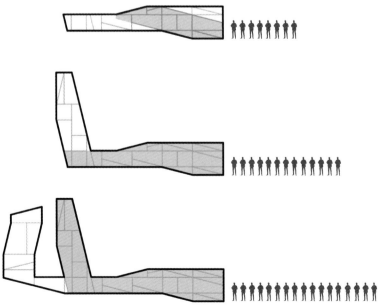

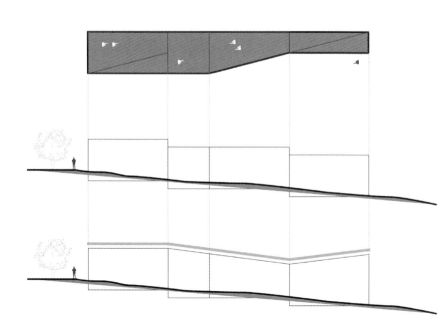

REVELATION

This pair of shelters offers rest and accommodation for pilgrims travelling the 117-kilometre journey for the adoration of the Virgin of Talpa through the Sierra Madre Occidental mountain range in Jalisco, Mexico.

2
Designed to blend into the landscape, the shelters are predominantly formed of adobe bricks made from soil gathered at the site.

3
Entry into the shelters is concealed in small alcoves off the main cobbled podium. The smaller Albergue Atenguillo shelter has a simple rectangular plan, while the Albergue Estanzuela is more sophisticated, with slightly chamfered sides.

4
In anticipation of possible future expansion, the shelters are based on a modular system that allows the structures to be expanded as necessary.

5
Both shelters are composed of one long room abutted by an ablution area. They are sited on hillsides and run perpendicular to the direction of the slope.

6
Appropriate to the surrounding landscape, the buildings sit low to the ground. Their elongated pentagonal forms are arranged end to end.

7
Shared spaces for pilgrims to gather include a large paved outdoor space and a small garden to the rear of the shelter.

6↑ 7↓

PILGRIM ROUTE SHELTERS   **Luis Aldrete**

Entrances to the shelter are differentiated from the interior by cobbled paving of local stone.

9
The open latticework allows breezes to blow through the structure and refresh the interior. These unglazed apertures also maintain a direct connection to the countryside beyond.

10
Adobe brick clay walls and clay lintels enclose the steel-framed structures, which have concrete roofs and paving tiles. The simple brick construction allows for gaps in the bond to be left at intervals that brings light into the interior and mitigates the harsh sunlight.

PILGRIM ROUTE SHELTERS   **Luis Aldrete**

The German art critic Gottfried Semper wrote of the distinction between the stereotomic – the cave-like buildings carved out of the earth and the ground – and the tectonic – the pieces of timber, stone and metal that were joined together and constructed by humans. It was, according to Semper, when these two elements met in tension that truly great architecture was made. This chapel, in the Los Andes Valley in Chile, can be seen as a perfect, modern-day encapsulation of Semper's ideal type. Partly submerged in earth, with a structure that hovers above its excavated underbelly, the building is an elegant marriage of technical construction and the clever inhabiting of elemental, earthly, spaces.

In Los Andes, Chile, 70 kilometres (43 miles)north of Santiago, the chapel stands out from the surrounding terrain, helped by a large elevated cross in the parking lot and the distinctiveness of its exterior. Yet it soon reveals itself to be also of the terrain. The building appears to have completely blank facades, with no doors or windows visible anywhere, with fins projecting from each of its four walls. Only when the visitor approaches the chapel is it revealed that the building's entrance takes one into the belly of the earth, down a ramp heading beneath the ground, where the congregation sits. What look like the building's walls turns out to be the building's superstructure, sitting above it, giving the chapel beneath a generously high volume.

The Capilla del Retiro chapel serves the pilgrims who journey to this site, to worship at the Sanctuary of Teresa de los Andes, next to the Carmelite Monastery of Auco. It is here and at the foot of Mount Carmelo that the Capilla del Retiro was built, next door to the guesthouse where visitors can stay. The pilgrims who visit come in search of transcendence, silence and reflection.

The main structure of the building is made of concrete. Four beams overlaid to make the shape of a cross extrude upwards to define the volume of the building's superstructure. This has minimal support from the ground, and sits only on four footings located at the corners that enable the structure to 'float' above the patio that was excavated beneath it. A thick, rustic stone wall was built around this excavation, and it rises around the perimeter of the chapel, echoing the hardy surrounding landscape. In dramatic contrast with this heavy stereotomy, glass panels stretch from the level of the raised concrete superstructure to the new ground datum of the building, creating a transparent 'skirt' that surrounds the bottom of the chapel.

The interior of the single-volume chapel introduces a third material, a wooden box, which creates the cladding of the interior of the chapel and its soffit. This timber is made from recycled railway sleepers, which introduces an element of age and historical continuity into an otherwise thoroughly modern project. The dim lighting of the interiors, coupled with the darkness of the timber, contrasts with the strong lighting coming in at ground level, helping to create an intimate and sombre atmosphere inside. This wooden box within the concrete superstructure hangs two metres beneath it, restricting the view outside, yet letting light into the building through the glass 'skirt'.

As well as the pleasing tensions between stereotomy and tectonics outlined above, the architects compare the ensemble to the duality typical in Gothic architecture, with a rational exterior enlivened by an interior that encourages reflection on the metaphysical. The effect is of a box that appears to levitate above the ground, barely tethered from taking off skywards, perhaps mirroring the souls of those who come to worship there.

CAPILLA DEL RETIRO

Undurraga Devés Arquitectos | Auco, Los Andes, Chile, 2009

CAPILLA DEL RETIRO Undurraga Deves Arquitectos

3↑　4↓

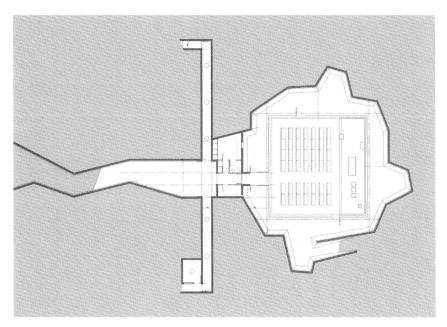

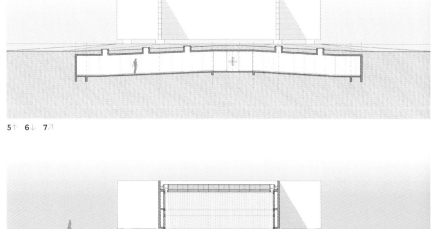

5↑　6↓　7↗

1
Excavated from the terrain and supported by a thick stone wall, the rustic chapel interior is lined with recycled railway line sleepers.

2
Visitors entering the chapel experience a contrast between the superstructure above, and a deep rocky cleft that leads to the subterranean belly.

3
From afar, a cross affixed to a pole is the only clue to the programme of the mysterious concrete building.

4
Plan: Excavated in an irregular faceted shape, the building and entry axis is composed in response to the location of existing facilities and the imposing landscape.

5
Long section: Raised on four concrete blocks, the pre-cast concrete walls appear to hover above the interior, excavated body of the church.

6
Cross section: The chapel is composed of three essential materials – the concrete superstructure at ground level, a rough rocky retaining wall, and the suspended, timber-lined interior.

7
At ground level, the concrete superstructure of four beams intersect to form an extruded cross and conceal the chapel below.

8

An interior of suspended timber lining is set within glass walls, which creates an illusion of a room suspended in a void. This inversion of traditional top-lit ecclesiastical spaces also shields the chapel from excessive sunlight.

9

The cold stone walls contrast with the warmth of reclaimed timber, heightening the distinction between inside and out, sacred and profane.

10

A foil to the rich, textural volume, the altar is simply composed of cast concrete elements. The gilded crucifix is the only overt reference to traditional, decorative Catholic spaces for worship.

11

Supported by a minimum of structural elements, the relationship between the smooth concrete planes and the earth is simple and essential. The deep rocky pit below sits in rough contrast, creating visual tension.

8↑   9↓

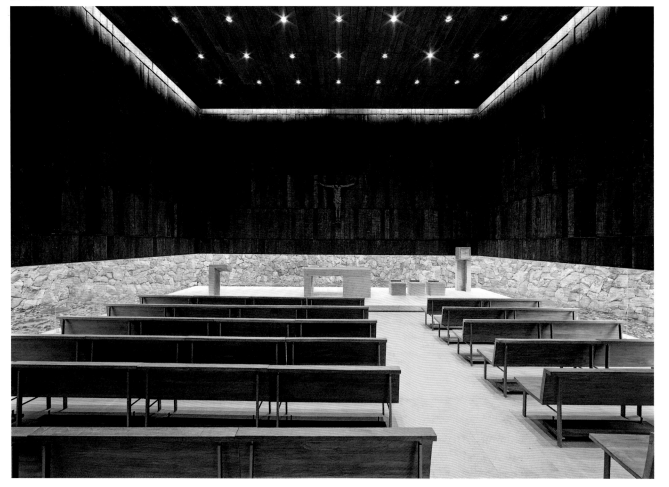

10↑ 11↓

CAPILLA DEL RETIRO   **Undurraga Deves Arquitectos**

Standing out from its low-rise neighbours in the waterside town of Kuokkala is what looks like an overgrown barn. This imposing building was another competition win for the Finnish practice Office for Peripheral Architecture who, in 2004, operating as Lassila Hirvilammi Architects, completed another striking church, the Kärsämäki Shingle Church (see page 28). The Kuokkala Church also makes use of locally sourced Finnish timber but uses more complex construction materials and building techniques than the hand-built church at Kärsämäki.

Jyväskylä is a busy city on the western edge of the Finnish lakeland region where some of Alvar Aalto's most celebrated architectural works can be found, including his Experimental House and the Säynätsalo Town Hall. In Kuokkala, the parish wanted a community hub but one which retained its identity as a place of worship. Its site, located in the market square and looking across to residential apartment buildings, lent itself to a church that could become a landmark for the area. The resulting church has a distinctive, chamfered mass to it, which neatly encloses the several function rooms over three storeys and a spectacular timber-lined nave and central worship space.

Rather than having a spire attached to the body of the church, the architects built a belvedere which sits in front of the church, strengthening its identity as a place of worship. The church's dislodged spire effectively creates a public square in front of the church, a small public space of a different kind to that created by the car parks and arcades of the nearby shopping malls and apartment blocks. The church's exterior space can accommodate spill-out from weddings or other ceremonies, but also provides an apron for the path that takes visitors around the side of the building and up a flight of Finnish granite steps to the first-floor main entrance. Once inside, the visitor can either go through to the body of the church to their right, or to the social rooms to the left. For flexibility, the church and parish meeting halls can be combined into one large sacral space that has adjoining youth facilities. A gallery between the halls houses the organ and the cantors' offices. The parish offices are downstairs, on the ground floor, and floor-to-ceiling windows and a door offer views of, and direct access to, the town's market square.

Inside, the soft, warm hues of Finnish spruce contrast with the exteriors. The roof and walls are clad in Spanish slate tiles, with timber and copper entrance details. The main vaulting structure of the nave comprises glu-laminated beams with a lattice-work of locally sourced spruce which sits beneath it, resembling the fine carpentry of a timber hulled boat. The nave is top-lit, with a large rooflight running the length of its apex. A vertical side window behind the altar casts light on to the chancel, to dramatic effect. Behind the altar there is an abstract timber sculpture that runs up the rear wall. Towards the rear of the nave is a gallery for the choir space, accessed by a spiral staircase encased in timber which, like the gallery, is painted white, a horizontal and spiral datum contrasting with the rest of the church. This gallery marks the point at which the church is at full capacity – which is when the congregation can sit behind it. Ordinarily, a smaller congregation sits in front of it. The furniture throughout is made in ash and lime wood and all the rooms are timber-lined and fitted with timber floors, creating a warm, intimate feel throughout. The effect is one of a contemporary cathedral, in which hand-crafts and local materials have been used together with the opportunities afforded by industrially produced timber beams.

KUOKKALA CHURCH
Office for Peripheral Architecture | Kuokkala, Jyväskylä, Finland, 2010

1↓   2→

KUOKKALA CHURCH **Office for Peripheral Architecture**

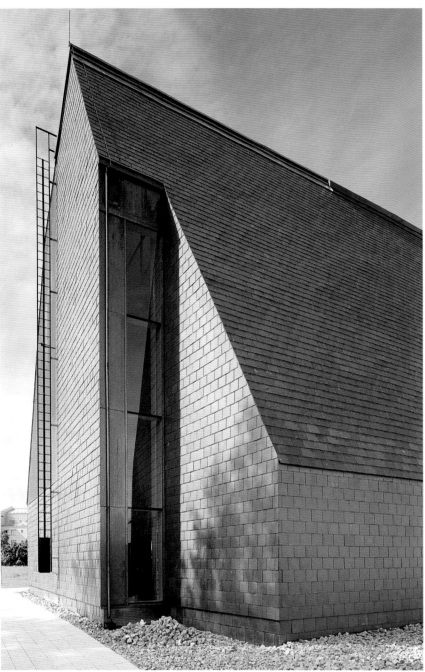

1

The significant, chamfered mass of the new church loosely references the typology of a barn. It serves as a point of contrast to the neighbouring apartments and market square.

2

A freestanding belvedere sits several metres away from the front of the church, strengthening its identity as a place of worship and forming a small plaza.

3

Clad in Spanish slate tiles, the distinction between walls and roof is blurred. The dark mass highlights copper and timber detailing of windows and doors.

4

Cross section: Choir stalls elevated above the central hall are positioned at the lower datum of the curved lattice lining.

5

Long section: The interior of the volume rises from a lower entrance to reach full height above the altar.

6

The predominant slate slope of the building falls away, towards the main entrance at first-floor level.

7

First floor plan: Suspended across the full width of the church, the choir stalls are accessed by a single spiral staircase.

8

Ground floor plan: Accommodating church and ancillary functions, visitors enter the building and can either proceed into the space for worship (right) or enter social areas (left).

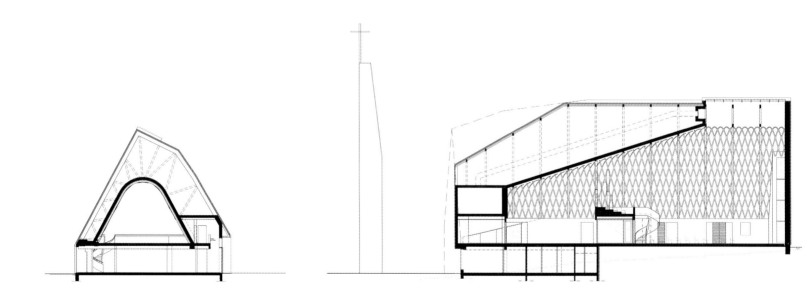

6↑ 7↓ 8↳

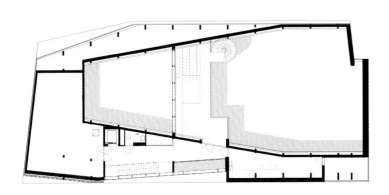

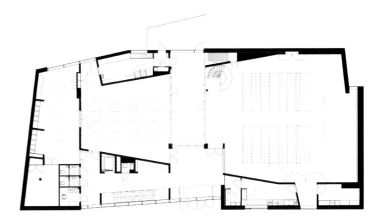

KUOKKALA CHURCH   **Office for Peripheral Architecture**

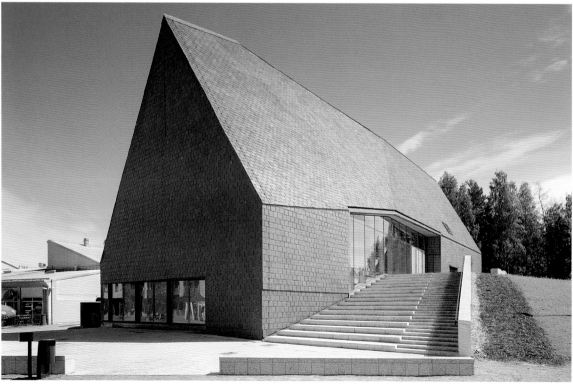

REVELATION

9
In contrast to the car parks and arcades of shopping malls nearby, the open public plaza in front of the church is delineated with granite paving and the distinctive asymmetric bell tower.

10
A broad flight of steps of Finnish granite leads visitors around the side of the building to the main entrance.

11
The church's exterior space can accommodate overspill from weddings or other ceremonies. Parish offices are located at the lower level; their full-height windows and a door offer transparency and give staff views and direct access to the market square.

12

Formed of glu-laminated beams with a latticework of locally sourced spruce beneath, the dramatic timber-lined interior creates an atmosphere of warmth. A window to the left of the altar highlights the chancel.

13

Encased in white-painted timber, the spiral staircase allows access to the choir stalls above. Its horizontal and spiral datum contrasts with the rest of the church.

14

A large rooflight running the full length of the nave casts shadows inside the generous volume, creating changing patterns on the walls and floor.

KUOKKALA CHURCH   **Office for Peripheral Architecture**

ARCHITECTS' BIOGRAPHIES

Luis Aldrete
www.luisaldrete.com

Luis Aldrete born in Guadalajara, Jalisco, Mexico | Lives and works in Mexico | Education Degree in Architecture, ITESO, 1995; Degree in Advanced Studies, Polytechnic University of Catalonia, 1999 | Recent works 2010: Pilgrim Route Shelters, Jalisco, Mexico; 2011: EPR House, Zapopan, Jalisco, Mexico; 2012: SC PTV House, Nayarit, Mexico; ECO Pavillion, Mexico City, Mexico; 2014: BF House, Borriol, Castellón de la Plana, Spain; Rinconada Margaritas Residential Buildings, Zapopan, Jalisco, Mexico | Recent publications 2009: A+U Architecture and Urbanism No. 480, Tokyo, Japan; 2010: Arquine 53; 2011: Architext; Achitektura & Biznes; 2012: Arquine 60; Rutas de Jaliso; Ruta del Peregrino a photographic essay by Iwan Baan; Naked Architecture; Indexnewspaper No. 1; Mexico Design; The New Mexico; 2013: Cutter Revista de Arquitectura y cultura; Mexico Design Elementals; Abitare No. 509 | Recent exhibitions 2012: Common Ground, La Biennale di Venezia; 2013: Mock Up of a Common Place, LIGA, Mexico; LIGA Mexico; Above MM, Mexico-Madrid; 2014: Iberoamerica-Arquitectura y Ciudad, Venezuela

PILGRIM ROUTES | SHELTERS
202—207

Region Jalisco, Mexico
Religion Christianity
Area 312 m² (3,360 sq ft; Estanzuela Shelter) and 618 m² (6,650 sq ft; Atenguillo Shelter)
Project team Magui Peredo, Cynthia Mojica

Andrea Dragoni Architetto + Francesco Pes
www.andreadragoni.it

Andrea Dragoni born in Perugia, 1969 | Lives and works in Perugia | Education Faculty of Architecture, University of Florence, 1997 | Recent works 2010: Public Spaces for Palazzo della Regione Friuli Venezia Giulia, Udine (with artist Nicola Renzi); 2011: Laboratory for Faculty of Pharmacy, Perugia (with P. Zannetti and P.A.Belli); Gubbio Cemetery, Umbria; 2012: Palazzo Senago, Senago-Milan; 2013: Images Theatre, touring exhibition for Steve McCurry/Sensational Umbria (with HOFLAB); Vidrala Complex, Milan; 2014: Exhibition gallery, Convento di San Francesco al Prato, Perugia | Recent publications 2014: Maurizio.Fagioli (ed.), 'Andrea Dragoni' in Figura e paesaggio nell'architetura italiana, Firenze, Aion Edizioni; Andrea Dragoni, 'Cielos de silencio' in Arquitectura Viva, Italy; Andrea Dragoni, 'Gubbio Cemetery extension', in C3, Korea | Recent exhibitions 2012: Emerging architecture, Royal Institute British Architects, London; La città dell'architettura, Palazzo Cordellina, Vicenza; 2013:Project Heracles, European Parliament, Brussels; 2014: 8° Biennal Internacional de Paisatge, Palau de la Música Catalana, Barcelona | 2012: AR+D Emerging Architecture Award (highly commended); 2013: Emirates Glass LEAF award (shortlist) 2014: Iconic Awards (Best of the Best); IQU Prize (Winner); Premio Minerva Etrusca per l'Archiettura

GUBBIO CEMETERY
154—159

Region Gubbio, Umbria, Italy
Religion Multifaith
Area 1,800 m² (19,375 sq ft)
Collaborators Andrea Moscetti Castellani, Giorgio Bettelli, Michela Donini, Raul Cambiotti, Antonio Ragnacci, Cristian Cretaro, Matteo Scoccia

Shigeru Ban
www.shigerubanarchitects.com

Shigeru Ban born in Japan, 1957 | Lives and works in Tokyo | Education Tokyo University of the Arts; Southern California Institute of Architecture, 1980; Cooper Union School of Architecture, 1984 | Recent works 2010: Centre Pompidou-Metz museum, Metz, France; 2013: Cardboard Cathedral, Christchurch, New Zealand; Yakushima Takatsuka Lodge, Kagoshima, Japan; Villa at Sengokuhara, Hakone, Japan; Shigeru Ban Paper Temporary Studio in Kyoto University of Art and Design; Kyoto; Abu Dhabi Art Pavilion, Abu Dhabi; 2014: Paper Nursery School, Ya'an, Sichuan, China; Paper Log House, Cebu, Philippines | Philip Jodidio, Shigeru Ban Complete Works 1985–2010, Taschen, Germany; 2011: Philip Jodidio, Shigeru Ban, Taschen; 2013: Shigeru Ban, How to Make Houses, Heibonsha, Japan; Shigeru Ban, NA Architects Series 07, Nikkei BP, Japan | Recent exhibitions 2013: The humanitarian adventure: Reducing Natural Risks, Red Cross Museum, Geneva, Switzerland | Japan; 2004: Prix de l'Académie d'Architecture de France; 2005: Arnold W. Brunner Memorial Prize in Architecture, American Academy of Arts and Letters, USA; 2009: Grand Prize, Architectural Institute of Japan; 2010: l'Ordre des Arts et des Lettres, France; 2011: National Order of Merit, France; Auguste Perret Prize for Technology Applied to Architecture; 2014: Pritzker Architecture Prize, USA

CARDBOARD CATHEDRAL
22—27

Region Christchurch, New Zealand
Religion Christianity
Area c.1,000 m² (c.10,760 sq ft)

Bayer & Strobel Architekten
www.bayerundstrobel.de

Gunther Bayer born 1971; Peter Strobel born 1975 | Live and work in Kaiserslautern, Germany | Education both studied Architecture at Kaiserslautern University of Technology | Founded Bayer & Strobel Architekten in 2006 | Recent works 2012: Clinical Pharmacy Mannheim, Germany; Ingelheim Funeral Chapel, Germany; House Z Frankfurt, Germany; 2014: Primary School Unterföhring, Germany; House on a Slope | Recent publications 2012: BDA-Preis Rheinland-Pfalz, Dölling und Galitz Verlag; 2013: Aus Allen Richtungen, Karl Krämer Verlag | Recent exhibitions 2013: Aus allen Richtungen. Positionen junger Architekten, Berlin; 2014: Stadtbaukunst – Der Stein in der Fassade, Dortmund | Awards 2008: DEUBAU-Preis for House W; 2012: Gold Winner, BDA-Preis RLP for Funeral Chapel Ingelheim; Best Architects 13 for Funeral Chapel Ingelheim; 2013: Gold Winner, Best Architects 14 for House Z; 2014: Silver Winner, Fritz-Höger prize for detached/semi-detached houses; Gold Winner, Bauherrenpreis 2014 Saarland, Architectural Association Saarland, for Bauservice Saarbrücken

INGELHEIM FUNERAL CHAPEL
166—173

Region Ingelheim am Rhein, Germany
Religion Christianity
Area 1,043 m² (11,225 sq ft)
Design team Gunther Bayer, Peter Strobel

Bernardo Bader Architekten
www.bernardobader.com

Bernardo Bader born 1974 | Lives and works in Austria | Education University of Innsbruck, 2001 | Recent works 2010: Behmann, Egg, Austria; House in the field, Sulz, Austria; 2012: Islamic Cemetery, Altach, Austria; Sauna House, Hohenems, Austria; 2013: House on the moor, Krumbach, Austria; 2014: Kindergarten Susi Weigel, Bludenz, Austria | Recent publications 2014: Häuser des Jahres, Calwey; Hide and Seek, Gestalten; Best of Detail: Holz/Wood; | Recent exhibitions 2013: Architecture is Life Aga Khan Prize for Architecture, Vorarberg Museum, Bregenz; Public Space Award, Chicago, New York, Barcelona | Awards 2012: 1st Prize, Piranesi Award; 2013: Aga Khan Award for Architecture; 2014: International Architecture Award

ISLAMIC CEMETERY
148—153

Region Altach, Austria
Religion Islam
Area 8,400 m² (90,400 sq ft)
Lead architect Sven Matt
Structural designer Merz Kley Partner ZT GmbH
Master builder Thomas Marte Baumeister
Construction company Hilti&Jehle
Carpentry Berchtold Holzbau

Beton
www.betonon.com

Founders Marta Rowińska and Lech Rowiński both born 1976 | Live and work in Poland | Education Rowińska: Faculty of Architecture, Warsaw University of Technology, 2001; Youth College of the Łódź Academy of Fine Arts, 2006. Rowiński: Faculty of Architecture, Warsaw University of Technology, 2001 | Beton founded, 2007 | Recent works 2009: Wooden Church, Tarnów, Poland; 2012: Triangular Cardboard Systems; 2013: Polish Design Focus (exhibition design), DMY, Berlin | Recent publications 2010: Closer to God, Gestalten; 2011: Wood Architecture Now!, Taschen; 2013: Wonder Wood, Birkhäuser | Recent exhibitions 2012: Tree Project, Municipal Art Gallery, Zakopane, Poland; Mies van der Rohe Award 2011, finalists' exhibition; Unpolished 15, National Museum of Contemporary Art, Bucharest; Common Roots, Design Museum, Holon, Israel; 2013: Young Creative Poland, London Design Festival; 2014: 5+ project – kids' playground at Gdynia Design Days; Błądzić jest rzeczą, BWA Tarnów

WOODEN CHURCH
34—39

Region Tarnów, Poland
Religion Christianity
Area 43 m² (460 sq ft)
Building team Local semi-professional builders

BNKR Arquitectura
www.bunkerarquitectura.com

Founder Esteban Suárez born in Mexico City, 1978 | Lives and works in Mexico City | Education Architecture and Urban Planning degree, Universidad Iberoamericana, 2004 | Recent works 2010: Hotel Filadelfia, Mexico City, Mexico; Hookah Lounge Satelite, Estado de Mexico, Mexico; 2011: Sunset Chapel, Guerrero, Mexico; 2012: Ecumenical Chapel, Morelos, Mexico | Recent publications 2010: BNKR, Stop: Keep Moving, Arquine; 2011: BNKR, Chapels, Mexican Editorial Arquine | Recent exhibitions 2012: Upcycling Pavilion, Expo CIHAC, Mexico City; 2013: Panel Rey Pavilion, Expo CIHAC, Mexico City; 2013: Social Typography, Chihuahua Book Fair, Mexico; Dogchitecture, Polyforum Siqueiros, Mexico City | Awards 2012: Best Commercial and Institutional Architecture under 1000 square metres, AZURE Awards, Toronto; 2013: Popular Choice Winner for Architecture +Self Initiated Projects, Architizer A+ Awards, New York; 2014: Iconic Awards, German Design Council; International Architecture Awards, The Chicago Athenaeun Museum of Architecture and Design

SUNSET CHAPEL
184—189

Region Acapulco, Mexico
Religion Christianity
Area 120 m² (1,290 sq ft)
Project team Mario Gottfried, Rodrigo Gil, Roberto Ampudia, Javier González, Óscar Flores, David Sánchez, Diego Eumir

Bureau SLA
www.bureausla.nl

Founder Peter van Assche born 1966 | Lives and works in Amsterdam | Education Academy of Architecture in Rotterdam, 2001 | Recent works 2010: National Glass Museum, Holland; 2012: Noorderparkbar, Amsterdam; 2013: Buddhist Meditation Centre Metta Vihara, the Netherlands; 2014: Dome Fort Asperen, the Netherlands

BUDDHIST MEDITATION CENTRE METTA VIHARA
86—91

Region Hengstdijk, the Netherlands
Religion Buddhism
Area 465 m² (5,005 sq ft)
Design team Peter van Assche, Hiske van der Meer, Gonçalo Moreira, Charlotte Vermaning, Justyna Osiecka
Contractor Van Kerckhoven Bouw, Kloosterzande
Structural Engineer Sineth Engineering, Schiphol
Sustainability: Sunraytec, Woerden

Kashef Chowdhury | URBANA
kashefchowdhury-urbana.com

Kashef Mahboob Chowdhury born in Dhaka, Bangladesh | Lives and works in Bangladesh | Education Bangladesh University of Engineering and Technology (BUET), 1995; Glenn Murcutt Masterclass, Sydney, 2006 | Recent works 2011: Bengal Art Lounge, Gulshan, Dhaka; Friendship Centre, Gaibandha, Bangladesh; 2013: Friendship Hospital, Satkhira, Bangladesh; EHL Premium Apartments, Gulshan, Dhaka; Museum of Independence and Independence Monument of Bangladesh, Dhaka, Bangladesh | Recent publications 2013: Catherine Slessor, ed., Kashef Chowdhury/URBANA, Architectural Review Special Monograph, London: Architectural Review | Recent exhibitions 2014: To Live Is To Be Slowly Born, Bengal Art Lounge, Dhaka | Awards 1996: First Prize, National Independence Monument Design Competition; 2010: Winner, Institute of Architects Bangladesh (IAB) Design Award, Bangladesh; 2012 First prize, Architectural Reviews's AR Emerging Architecture Award, UK; 2013: Winner, Architect of the Year Award (AYA) for Focus Countries, India

CHANDGAON MOSQUE
68—73

Region Chittagong, Bangladesh
Religion Islam
Area 1,048 m² (11,280 sq ft)

Claus van Wageningen Architecten

www.clausvanwageningen.nl

Felix Claus born 1956; Dick van Wageningen born 1971 | Felix Claus lives in Amsterdam, Paris and Tokyo; Dick van Wageningen lived in Breukelen; both work in Amsterdam | Education Felix Claus: Diploma in Architecture, Delft University of Technology, 1987 | Recent works 2004: Fire Station, Utrecht; Townhall, Tynaarlo; 2006: Church, Rijsenhout; Townhall, Library and Theatre, Nijverdal; 2007: De Eekenhof, Enschede; 2008: Office IJburg, Amsterdam; 2009: Private House Steigereiland, Amsterdam; 2011: Netherlands Institute for Ecology, Wageningen, Netherlands; 2012: Central Fine Collection Agency, Leeuwarden, Netherlands; 2014: National Military Museum, Soesterberg

DUTCH REFORMED CHURCH
120—125

Region Rijsenhout, the Netherlands
Religion Christianity
Area 878 m² (9,450 sq ft)
Project Team Jan Kerkhoff, Stefan Hofschneider, Leo van den Burg, James Webb

Itami Jun Architects

www.itmarch.com

Itami Jun 1937–2011 | Education B.Arch, Musashi Institute of Technology, 1968 | Recent works 2007: Duson Art Museum, Jeju, Korea; Town House, Yangji, Korea; 2008: Atelier ITM, Bangbae-dong, Seoul; Godo Building, Jeokseon-dong, Seoul; O'Phel Golf Club House, Yeongcheon, Korea; 2009: Oboe Hills, Pyeongchang-dong, Seoul; Church of Water and Light, Jeju, Korea | Recent publications 2008: Jun Itami 1970-2008, Shufunotomo | Recent exhibitions 2002: Itami Jun, a Korean architect in Japan, Musée national des arts asiatiques-Guimet, Paris; 2010: CONTEMPLATING THE VOID: Interventions in the Guggenheim Museum, Guggenheim Museum, New York | Awards 2005: Chevalier de l'Ordre des arts et des Lettres; 2006: Kim Swoo-Geun Cultural Award; 2010: Murano Togo Award

CHURCH OF WATER AND LIGHT
92—97

Region Seojupo, Jeju Island, South Korea
Religion Christianity
Area 62 m² (663 sq ft)

Jun Aoki & Associates

www.aokijun.com

Jun Aoki born in Yokohama, Japan, 1956 | Lives and works in Tokyo | Education Bachelor of Engineering in Architecture, 1980; Master of Engineering in Architecture, 1982 | Recent works 2006: The Aomori Museum of Art, Aomori, Japan; 2010: Maison AoAo, Japan; 2011: Louis Vuitton Fukuoka Tenjin, Fukuoka, Japan; 2012: House m, Japan; 2013: L'Avenue Shanghai, Shanghai, China; Louis Vuitton, Matsuya Ginza, Tokyo, Japan; 2014: Omiyamae Gymnasium, Tokyo, Japan; Miyoshi City Hall, Hiroshima, Japan | Recent publications 2013: Jun Aoki, Jun Aoki Notebooks, Heibonsha | Recent exhibitions 2006: Taro Nasu Bambi, Osaka, Japan; 2009: Midsummer Plants, Tokyo, Japan; 2011: Okamura Design Space R Exhibition 9: "BOYOYONG", Tokyo, Japan; 2013: Red and Blue Line, Aichi, Japan | Awards 1997: The 13th Yoshioka Award; 2000: The Grand Award, The Aomori Museum of Fine Art (provisional class) Architectural Competition; 2004: The 11th Aichi Townscape Award; 2005: The Minister of Education's Art Encouragement Prize; 2008: Good Design Gold Award

WHITE CHAPEL
80—85

Region Osaka, Japan
Religion Christianity
Area 263 m² (2,830 sq ft)
Executive architect ATELIER G&B Corp.
Textile designer Yuko Aondo
Lighting engineer Izumi OKayasu

Katsuhiro Miyamoto & Associates
www.kmaa.jp

Katsuhiro Miyamoto born in Hyogo, Japan, 1961 | Lives and works in Japan | Education Bachelor of Architecture, University of Tokyo, 1984; Master of Architecture, 1987 | Recent works 2010: bird house, Aichi, Japan; 2012: Face of HOR-AIKAN, Iwate, Japan; 2013: Shinpuku-ji Temple Reception Hall, Nagano, Japan | Recent publications 2010: Katsuhiro Miyamoto, Grown, flick studio.co.,ltd; 2012: Dana Buntrock, Katsuhiro Miyamoto, Libria | Recent exhibitions 2013: Eastern Promise, Vienna, Austria; How did Architects Respond Immediately after 3/11 – The Great East Japan Earthquake, world tour | Awards 1998: Young Architect of the Year, Japan Institute of Architects; 2008: Grand Prize, Japan Commercial Environment Designers Association Design Award; 2010: Grand Prize, Japan Federation of Architects & Building Engineers Association Awards

CHUSHIN-JI TEMPLE PRIEST'S QUARTERS
196—201

Region Honshu, Nagano, Japan
Religion Buddhism
Area 243 m² (2,615 sq ft)
Project team Isamu Tamaishi, Takenori Uotani
Structural engineering Hirokazu Toki / University of Shiga Prefecture & Takashi Manda / Takashi Manda structural design

Mancini Enterprises
www.mancini-design.in

Founded 2004, Chennai, India | Founders J. T. Arima and Niels Schoenfelder | Education J. T. Arima: B. Arch., Goa; Niels Schoenfelder: Architecture Diploma, Technical University of Darmstadt | Recent works 2011: The Dune, Tamil Nadu, India; Elephant Valley, Western Ghats, India; Le Dupleix, Tamil Nadu, India; 2013: Crematorium for G.K.D. Charity Trust, Coimbatore, India; School for Children of the world, India; S8, south India; Landscape and Garden Room; Ingadi | Awards 2013: Best Architecture Single Residence, India, Asia Pacific Property Awards; 2014: AD50, India, The 50 most influential names in Indian architecture and design

CREMATORIUM FOR G.K.D. CHARITY TRUST
174—179

Region Coimbatore, Tamil Nadu, India
Religion Multifaith
Area 4,856 m² (52,270 sq ft)
Design team Niels Schoenfelder, J.T. Arima, Bharath Ram K, Ganesh V, Priyanka Rao, Sridharan A, Rijesh K, Divya K.N.

Nómena Arquitectos + Ximena Alvarez
www.nomena-arquitectos.com

Founders all born in Lima: Hector Loli in 1982; Jorge Sanchez in 1982; Moris Fleischman in 1979; Diego Franco in 1982 | All live and work in Lima | Education 2006: Founders completed studies at the Universidad Peruana de Ciencias Aplicadas; 2012: Founders completed masters degrees in London and Madrid | Recent works 2010: De La Piedra Chapel, Cieneguilla, Lima, Peru; 2013: Tent House, Cañete, Lima; Cube House, Punta Negra, Lima, Peru; 2014: Archipelago House, Vichayito, Peru; Lima Villa College, Peru; Villa Miermana, Chorrillos, Lima, Peru | Recent publications 2013: Nómena, ConPosiciones: 20 Approaches to Peruvian Architecture, YoPublico | Recent exhibitions 2011: Lima 100% Arquitectura, Colegio Oficial de Arquitectos de Madrid, Spain; 2012: Yucun: Inhabit the Desert, XIII International Biennale of Architecture, Venice, Italy | Awards 2010: Honorable Mention, XVII Bienal Panamericana de Arquitectura, Quito, Ecuador; Winner, XIV Bienal Nacional de Arquitectura del Peru, Lima, Peru; 2011: Third Place, Obra del Año 2010, Plataforma Arquitectura, Santiago, Chile; 2012: Selected Publication, Con_Posiciones, VIII Bienal Iberoamericana de Arquitectura y Urbamismo, Cádiz, Spain; 2014: Selected Work, Lima Villa College, IX Bienal Iberoamericana de Arquitectura y Urbanismo, Cádiz, Spain

DE LA PIEDRA CHAPEL
40—45

Region Cieneguilla, Peru
Religion Christianity
Area 85 m² (915 sq ft)
Lead architects Héctor Loli and Ximena Alvarez
Contractor Americo Chavez
Structure Luis Yeckle

OOPEAA
Office for Peripheral Architecture
oopeaa.com

Founder Anssi Lassila born in Soini, Finland, 1973 | Lives and works in Seinäjoki and Helsinki, Finland | Education Department of Architecture, University of Oulu, 2002 | Recent works 2010: Sauna Tonttu, Soini, Finland; 2013: Kompassi Block, Vaasa, Finland; 2014: House Riihi, Alajärvi, Finland | Recent publications 2014: Julie Cirelli, OOPEAA: Office for Peripheral Architecture, Arvinius + Orfeus Publishing | Recent exhibitions 2013: Nordic Cool, Washington DC, USA; Two Paths to Silence, Museum of Finnish Architecture; 2013–2014: Re-Creation, Architecture Biennale, Shenzen, China and Venice, Italy; 2014: Suomi Seven, Emerging Architects from Finland, Deutches Architektur Museum, Frankfurt; Materiality and the Magic of Light, Deutsche Gesellschaft für christliche Kunst Galerie, Munich; A New Generation of Wood Architecture, Museum of Finnish Architecture, Helsinki | Awards 2011: Red Dot Design Award; Arkitekturmässan Awards; Mies van der Rohe Award

KÄRSÄMÄKI SHINGLE CHURCH
28—33

Region Kärsämäki, Finland
Religion Christianity
Area 220 m² (2,370 sq ft)
Lead architect Anssi Lassila
Engineering Jussi Tervaoja

KUOKKALA CHURCH
214—221

Region Kuokkala, Jyväskylä, Finland
Religion Christianity
Area 1,311 m² (14,110 sq ft)
Lead architect Anssi Lassila
Collaborators Virve Väisänen, Juha Pakkala, Janne Kähkönen, Matias Topi, Yoshimasa Yamada

O Studio Architects
www.ostudioarchitects.com

Founder Fai Au born in Guangzhou, China, 1976 | Lives and works in Hong Kong | Education BA (Hons) in Architecture, Royal Melbourne Institute of Technology; Master of Art in Philosophy, Chinese University of Hong Kong; Master in Design Studies, Harvard University Graduate School of Design | O Studio Architects founded in 2009 | Recent works 2009: Mountain Water Gate, Huizhou, China; Luofu Mountain Museum, Huizhou, China | Recent publications 2012: Concrete Architecture and Design, Braun Publishing AG; 2013: Architecture Now! Vol. 9, Taschen; Interdisciplinary Design: New Lessons from Architecture and Engineering, Harvard GSD & Actar | Recent exhibitions 2011: HKIA Annual Award Exhibition; 2013: Agoras Guangzhou Green Architecture Exhibition | Awards 2011: Medal of the Year; 2011 HKIA Annual Award for Projects outside Hong Kong; Winner, 2011 World Architecture Community award; Winner, 2012 Perspective 40 under 40 Award; Young Architecture Prize, 2014 Chivas 18 Architecture and Design Awards

CHURCH OF SEED
46—51

Region Mount Luofu, China
Religion Christianity
Area 280 m² (3,010 sq ft)
Structure and M&E Consultant Guangzhou Architectural Engineering Design Institute
Main contractor Maoming Construction Group Co. Ltd.

Otxotorena Arquitectos
www.otxotorenaarquitectos.com

Founder Juan M. Otxotorena born in San Sebastian, Spain, 1959 | Lives and works in Pamplona, Spain | Education The University of Navarra, 1983 | Recent works 2011: Mendillorri High School, Navarra, Spain; Munabe Sport Track Cover, Loiu, Vizcaya; Water Treatment Station, Benidorm, Alicante; Valle de Egüés Town Hall, Sarriguren, Navarra; 2012: Economics & Masters Building, Campus University of Navarra, Spain; Tudela Courts, Navarra; 2013: New Buildings in Redin School, Pamplona, Spain; High School Ezkaba, Pamplona, Spain; COAS Offices and Headquarters, Loiu, Vizcaya; 2014: Center for Psychosocial Rehabilitation, Alicante, Spain | Recent publications 2013: Pedro Pegenaute, 'Juan M. Otxotorena Economics Building of the University of Navarra 2012', Photovolumes 1, Barcelona; 'Juan M. Otxotorena Edificio de Económicas y Masters de la Universidad de Navarra en Pamplona', Arquitecturas Singulares AASS 01/2013, T6 Ediciones, Pamplona; 2010: Juan M. Otxotorena, Arquitectura 2000/10 TC Cuadernos No. 95, Ediciones Dédalo

SHRINE OF THE VIRGIN OF LA ANTIGUA
52—57

Region Alberite, La Rioja, Spain
Religion Christianity
Area 122 m² (1,300 sq ft)
Lead architect Juan M. Otxotorena
Collaborator architects Andrés Ayesa, Carlos Díaz
Structural engineer Fernando Sarría
Construction company José Luis Sáenz Ausejo

John Pawson
www.johnpawson.com

John Pawson born in Halifax, Yorkshire, 1949 | Lives and works in London | Education Eton and Architectural Association | Recent works 2011: Casa delle Bottere, Treviso, Italy; 2012: Syukou Fujisawa Gallery and Café, Okinawa, Japan; 2013: Palmgren House, Drevviken, Sweden; Picornell House, Mallorca, Spain; St Tropez Houses, Provence, France; Montauk House, Long Island, USA | Recent publications 2010: Alison Morris, John Pawson Plain Space, Phaidon Press; 2011: El Croquis 158, John Pawson 2006–2011: the voice of matter, El Croquis Editorial, Spain; 2012: John Pawson, A Visual Inventory, Phaidon Press | Recent exhibitions 2010: Plain Space Exhibition, Design Museum, London; 2012: John Pawson Exhibition, Pinakothek der Moderne, Munich, Germany | Awards 2008: RIBA Stephen Lawrence Prize; Frate Sole International Prize for Sacred Architecture; 2014: Interior Designers of the Year, The German Design Council

ST MORITZ CHURCH
74—79

Region Augsburg, Bavaria, Germany
Religion Christianity
Area 1,857 m² (20,000 sq ft)
Lead architect Jan Hobel

Randić Turato
www.randic-turato.hr

Saša Randić born in Rijeka, Croatia, 1964 and Idis Turato born in Rijeka, Croatia, 1965 | Education Saša Randić: Faculty of Architecture, University of Zagreb, 1990 and Masters in Architecture, Berlage Institute, 1992; Idis Turanto: Faculty of Architecture, University of Zagreb, 1991 and Masters in Architecture, 2004 | Recent works 2003: Novigrad Lapidarium, Novigrad; Faculty of Technology, Rijeka; 2005: Elementary School Fran Krsto Frankopan and Kindergarden Katarina Frankopan, Krk; 2007: Zagrad Centre, Rijeka | Recent publications 2000: Various authors, Randić Turato–Architecture of Transition, Architekts, Croatia; 2006: Saša Randić and Idis Turato, In-Between: A book on the Croatian coast, global processes, and how to live with them, Actar; 2011: Ivan Rupnik, Transitional Moments, Actar | Recent Exhibitions 2005: International Architecture Biennale, Rotterdam; 2006: Croatian Pavilion, 10th International Architecture Biennale, Venice; 2007: Mies van der Rohe EU Prize for Architecture selection; 2009: Mies van der Rohe EU Prize for Architecture | Awards 2004: Viktor Kovacić Award, Croatia; 2005: Piranesi Award, Slovenia; 2006: Vladimir Nazor State Prize, Croatia; 2007: Selected, European Union Prize for Contemporary Architecture; Mies van der Rohe Award; 2008: Nominated, Swiss Architectural Award

POPE JOHN PAUL II HALL
190—195

Region Rijeka, Croatia
Religion Christianity
Area 1,048 m² (11,280 sq ft)
Project team Sinisa Glusica, Gordan Resan, Iva Cuzela-Bilac, Ana Stanicic (Technical Architects)
Contractor Aljosa Travas

Stanley Saitowitz | Natoma Architects
www.saitowitz.com

Stanley Saitowitz born in Johannesburg, South Africa, 1949 | Lives and works in San Francisco, USA | Education Bachelor of Architecture, University of Witwatersrand, 1974; Masters in Architecture, University of California, Berkeley, 1977 | Recent works 2011: W Hotel, San Francisco, California; 2012: Uptown Phase I, Cleveland Ohio; Accent, Cleveland, Ohio; 2013: 616 20th Street, San Francisco, California; 2014: Blanc, San Francisco, California; 8 Octavia, San Francisco, California; 1515 South Van Ness, San Francisco, California; Uptown Phase II, Cleveland, Ohio | Recent publications 2005: Stanley Saitowitz, Stanley Saitowitz: Buildings and Projects, Monacelli Press | Recent exhibitions 2012/2013: The Judaica Collection, Contemporary Jewish Museum | Awards 1997: Harleston Parker Medal; 2005: AIA SF Honor Award; 2007: AIA SF Design Awards; AIA SF Honor and Merit Awards; 2008: AIA SF Honor and Merit Awards; 2009: AIA SF Honor and Merit Awards; 2010: Citation and Honor Award in Architecture, AIA SF Design awards; 2014 Honor Award in Architecture, AIA SF Design awards

BETH SHOLOM SYNAGOGUE
108—113

Region San Francisco, California, USA
Religion Judaism
Area 2,694 m² (29,000 sq ft)
Project team Stanley Saitowitz, Neil Kaye, Markus Bischoff, John Winder, Derrick Chan
Structural engineering Forrell/Elsesser Engineers Inc.
Mechanical engineering Rumsey Engineers Inc.

SeARCH
www.search.nl

Bjarne Mastenbroek born in the Netherlands, 1964 | Lives and works in Amsterdam | Architecture diploma, Delft University of Technology, with honourable mention, 1989 | Recent works 2009: Forest Tower, Landgoed Schovenhorst, Putten; Villa Vals, Switzerland; City Villa, Museumlaan, Enschede; De Meester residences, Amsterdam; Zuidwest, Housing, Den Haag; 2010: Trefpunt Community Center, Marken; 'Eat Me' restaurant, interiors & renovation, Amsterdam; Mercatorplein Pavilion, Amsterdam; 2012: Kop van Kessel-Lo, development area central station, Leuven; Zuidas kiosk, Amsterdam; Learning Cluster, Oosterheem, Zoetermeer; Novo Nordisk Conference and Activity Center, Hillerød; 2013: Amsterdam Marina, Amsterdam; Isbjerget, Aarhus; 2014: Geert Groote College, Amsterdam; Het Nieuwe Paviljoen; Yourtopia, Rotterdam | Recent publications 2009: SeARCH, C3 Publishing Co., Seoul, Korea | Recent exhibitions 2012: 9 architects / 9 proposals to live, Villa Noailles, Hyères, France; Synagogues in the Netherlands, Delft; The Dutch Way of Housing the Crowd, Erasmus Huis, Jakarta Architecture Triennale; Architecture & Design Film Festival, Tribeca Cinemas, New York; Future City, Arnhem; 2013: Architecture the Dutch Way 1945–2000, the Hermitage, St Petersburg; Oslo Architecture Triennale, Oslo; Stad van Nederland, Nai, Rotterdam; "New message from the Neherlands", Korea Foundation Cultural Center Gallery, Seoul; 2014: Hout, HNI, Rotterdam; Behind the Green Door (Oslo Architecture Triennale), Danish Architecture Centre; Lookout. Architecture with a view, Swiss Architecture Museum | Awards 2010: Brick Award; 2011: Golden medal, Amsterdam Architecture Prize; Wallpaper* Design Award; 2013: MIPIM Award, Best Residential Development

LJG SYNAGOGUE
132—137

Region Amsterdam, the Netherlands
Religion Judaism
Area 3,400 m² (36,600 sq ft)
Project design Bjarne Mastenbroek & Uda Visser

Studio Tamassociati
www.tamassociati.org

Partners: Massimo Lepore born in Udine, 1960; Raul Pantaleo born in Milan, 1962; Simone Sfriso born in London, 1966 | All live and work in Italy | Education All graduated from IUAV Venice University | Recent works 2010: Outpatient Clinic, Marghera, Venice; 2011: Paediatric Centre Nyala, South Darfur, Sudan; Banca Popolare Etica Headquarters, Padua, Italy; 2012: Paediatric Centre Port Sudan, Sudan; 2014: Cohousing Mura San Carlo, Bologna, Italy; Cohousing Quattro Passi, Treviso, Italy | Recent publications 2013: Simone Sfriso and Edoardo Narne, L'abitare condiviso, Marsilio; Raul Pantaleo and Luca Molinari, Architetture Resistenti, Becco Giallo; AFRITECTURE – Building Social Change, Munich; 2014: Africa – Big Change, Big Chance, Triennale di Milano, Milan | Awards 2013: Aga Khan Award for Architecture; Curry Stone Design Prize; Giancarlo Ius Gold Medal; 2014: Zumtobel Group Award

PRAYER AND MEDITATION PAVILION
142—147

Region Khartoum, Sudan
Religion Multifaith
Area 65 m² (700 sq ft)
Site engineers Roberto Crestan (EMERGENCY NGO)
Program coordinator Pietro Parrino (EMERGENCY NGO)

Toyo Ito & Associates, Architects
www.toyo-ito.co.jp

Toyo Ito born in Seoul, Korea, 1941 | Lives and works in Tokyo | Education Department of Architecture, The University of Tokyo, 1969 | Recent works 2010: Torres Porta Fira, Barcelona, Spain; Belle Vue Residences, Singapore; 2011: Taipei World Trade Centre Square Landscape Design, Taipei, Taiwan; Toyo Ito Museum of Architecture, Imabari, Japan; Ken Iwata Mother and Child Museum, Imabari, Japan; Tokyo Gas Ei-Walk Concept Room, Arakawa-ku, Tokyo, Japan; Tokyo Mother's Clinic, Setagaya-ku, Tokyo, Japan; Yaoko Kawagoe Museum, Saitama, Japan; 2013: Hermès Pavilion, Basel, Switzerland | Recent publications 2009: Toyo Ito, Toyo Ito, Phaidon Press; El Croquis 147, Toyo Ito 2005–2009: liquid space, El Croquis Editorial, Spain; a+u 10:01 #472 Feature: Toyo Ito / Architecture and Place, A+U, Tokyo; 2010: Hsieh Tsungche, Pioneer Forever: The Great Architect Toyo Ito, Bookzone, Taiwan | Awards 1992: 33rd Mainichi Art Award; 1999: Japan Art Academy Prize; 2000: The Arnold W. Brunner Memorial Prize in Architecture; 2002: Golden Lion for Lifetime Achievement, 8th International Architecture Exhibition at Venice Biennale; 2003: Architectural Institute of Japan Prize; 2006: Royal Gold Medal from The Royal Institute of British Architects; 2008: ADI Compasso d'Oro Award; 2010: The Asahi Prize; 2012: Golden Lion for Best National Participation for the Japan Pavilion, 13th International Architecture Exhibition at Venice Biennale; 2013: Pritzker Architecture Prize

MEISO NO MORI
MUNICIPAL FUNERAL HALL
62—67

Region Kakamigahara, Gifu, Japan
Religion Multifaith
Area 2,269 m² (24,400 sq ft)
Structural engineers Sasaki Structural Consultants
Mechanical engineers Kankyo Engineering Inc.
Landscape design Mikiko Ishikawa

+udeb arquitectos
www.felipeuribedebedout.com

Founder Juan Felipe Uribe de Bedout born in Colombia, 1963 | Lives and works in Colombia | Education Universidad Pontificia Bolivariana, 1990 | Recent works 2010: Apartamento Astorga Loft; Apartamento Hoyos; Apartamento Torres Bosque Izquierdo; Casa Andrade; Casa en el Arbol; Estudio UdeB Bodega, Medellín, Colombia; Estudio UdeB Viscaya | Recent publications 2010: Felipe Hernández, Beyond Modernist Masters: Contemporary Architecture in Latin America, Birkhäuser GmbH | Awards 2000: First place Marble Architectural Awards (MAA), IMM Carrara, Italy; Asocreto Concrete Excellence Award

RITUALS CREMATORIUM
114—119

Region Guarne, Colombia
Religion Multifaith
Area 700 m² (7,500 sq ft)
Lead architect Juan Felipe Uribe de Bedout

Undurraga Devés Arquitectos
www.undurragadeves.cl

Founder Cristián Undurraga born in Santiago, Chile, 1954 | Lives and works in Chile | Education Catholic University of Chile, 1977 | Recent works 2010: Museum of Solidarity, Father Hurtado, Santiago, Chile; 2011: Ruca Dwellings, Santiago, Chile | Awards 2004: Gold Medal, Miami Biennale; International award, Ibero-American Biennale of Architecture and Urbanism; 2010: Ibero-American Biennale of Architecture and Urbanism 2012: Frate Sole International Award for Sacred Architecture, for Capilla del Retiro

CAPILLA DEL RETIRO
208—213

Region Auco, Los Andes, Chile
Religion Christianity
Area 620 m² (6,670 sq ft)
Design team Undurraga Deves Arquitectos, Cristián Larraín Bontá, Pablo López, Jean Baptiste Bruderer
Altar design José Vicente Gajardo
Structural engineer José Jiménez, Rafael Gatica Engineers
Constructor Terrano S.A.

Wandel Hoefer Lorch Architekten
www.wandel-hoefer-lorch.de

Wolfgang Lorch born in Nürtingen am Necker, Germany, 1960; Andrea Wandel born Saarbrücken, Germany, 1963 | Both live and work in Germany | Wolfgand Lorch and Andrea Wandel: Architecture diploma, TU Darmstadt, 1990 | Recent works 2010: Hybrid Highrise, Tbilisi, Georgia; 2011: St. John Parish Centre, Neunkirchen, Germany; 2012: Ecumenical Forum HafenCity, Hamburg, Germany; 2011: St. John Parish Centre, Neunkirchen, Germany | 2007: Ready for Take Off, VII International Architecture Biennial, São Paulo; 2008: Germany Architecture Yearbook 2008/2008, Deutsches Architekturmuseum, Frankfurt am Main; Ready for Take Off, Deutsches Architekurmuseum | 2006: Mention, Deutscher Stahlbaupreis, Germany; 2007: Preis des Deutschen Architekturmuseums; 2007: Deutscher Naturstein Preis, Germany; 2008: Recognition, Balthaser-Neumann Preis, Germany; Deutscher Städtebaupreis, Germany

JEWISH COMMUNITY CENTRE, SYNAGOGUE AND MUSEUM
102—107

Region Munich, Germany
Religion Judaism
Area 11,890 m² (128,000 sq ft)
Structural planner Sailer Stepan und Partner GmbH

Kris Yao | Artech

www.krisyaoartech.com

Kris Yao born Taipei, Taiwan, 1951 | Lives and works in Taiwan | Education Bachelor of Architecture, Tunghai University, 1975; Master of Architecture, University of California, Berkeley, 1978 | Recent works 2010: Lanyang Museum, Yilan County, Taiwan; 2012: Water-Moon Monastery, Neihu District, Taiwan; 2013: Wuzhen Theater, Cechiang, China; China Steel Corporation Headquarters, Taiwan; Shinkong Xinyi Office Tower, Taipei City, Taiwan | Recent publications 2010: Architecture of Kris Yao | Artech, The Images Publishing Group Pty Ltd, Australia | Recent exhibitions 2013: Atlas of the Unbuilt World, International Architecture Showcase (IAS), London, United Kingdom; 2014: Time Space Existence – The Ninth Column, 14th La Biennale di Venezia, Venice, Italy | Awards 1997: Chinese Outstanding Architect Award; 2005: Distinguished Alumni Award from the College of Environmental Design, UC Berkeley, California; 2007: National Award for Arts, Taiwan; 2014: Honorary Fellowship of the American Institute of Architects

WATER-MOON MONASTERY

160—165

Region Taipei, Taiwan
Religion Buddhism
Area 27,936 m² (300,700 sq ft)
Design team Hua-Yi Chang, Kuo-Lung Lee, Wen-Li Liu, Jen-Ying Kuo, Yvonne Lee, Chin Tai, Jun-Ren Chou, Yi-Heng Lin, David Chang

Peter Zumthor

Peter Zumthor born in Basel, Switzerland, 1943 | Lives and works in Switzerland | Education Arts and Crafts School, Basel 1963–67; Pratt Institute, New York, USA, 1966 | Recent works 2011: Steilneset Memorial, Vardo, Norway; Serpentine Gallery Pavilion, London, United Kingdom; 2012: Werkraumhaus, Andelsbuch, Austria | Recent publications 2010: Peter Zumthor, Thinking Architecture, 3rd edition, Birkhäuser; 2014: Peter Zumthor, Buildings and Projects. 1985–2013, ed. by Thomas Durisch, Scheidegger & Spiess. | Awards 1998: Carlsberg Architecture Prize in Denmark; Mies van der Rohe Award for European Architecture; 2006: Thomas Jefferson Foundation Medal in architecture; 2008: Prix Meret Oppenheim, Federal Office of Culture, Switzerland; 2008: DAM Prize of Architecture, Germany; Arnold W. Brunner Memorial Prize; Praemium Imperiale from the Japan Art Association; 2009: The Pritzker Architecture Prize; 2013: RIBA Royal Gold Medal

BROTHER KLAUS FIELD CHAPEL

126—131

Region Mechernich, Germany
Religion Christianity

BIBLIOGRAPHY

Ruthven, Malise
Islam: A Very Short Introduction
(New York, Oxford University Press, 2000)

Stierlin, Henri
Islam: Early Architecture from Baghdad to Cordoba
(Cologne and New York, Taschen, 2002)

Le Corbusier
Towards a New Architecture tr. Frederick Etchells
(Oxford Architectural Press, 1997)

Curl, James S and Sambrook, John J
A Dictionary of Architecture
(Oxford and New York, Oxford University Press, 2000)

Ghirardo, Diane Y
Architecture after Modernism
(New York, Thames and Hudson, 1996)

Hillenbrand, Robert, *Islamic Art and Architecture*
(New York, Thames and Hudson, 1999)

Vardey, Lucinda
God in All Worlds: An Anthology of Contemporary Spiritual Writing
(London, Chatto & Windus, 1995)

Britton, Karla, ed.
Constructing the Ineffable: Contemporary Sacred Architecture
(New Haven, Yale School of Architecture, 2010)

Heathcote, Edwin, and Moffatt, Laura
Contemporary Church Architecture
(Chichester, Wiley-Academy, 2007)

Heathcote, Edwin
Monument Builders: Modern Architecture and Death
(London, Academy Editions, 1999)

Bauman, Zygmunt
Liquid Modernity
(Cambridge, Polity Press, 2000)

Wilson, Bryan
Religion in Sociological Perspective
(Oxford, Oxford University Press, 1981)

Hugh McLeod and Werner Ustorf, eds.
The Decline of Christendom in Western Europe, 1750–2000,
(Cambridge, Cambridge University Press, 2003)

Berger, Peter L
The Heretical Imperative: Contemporary Possibilities of Religious Affirmation
(Garden City, NY, Anchor Press, 1979)

Berger, Peter L
'The Secularism in Retreat' in *The National Interest* 46
(Winter 1996–97)

Durkheim, Émile
The Elementary Forms of the Religious Life
(Oxford, Oxford University Press, 2001)

Semper, Gottfried
Style in the Technical and Tectonic Arts; or, Practical Aesthetics
(Los Angeles, Getty Research Institute, 2004)

Frampton, Kenneth
Modern Architecture: A Critical History
(London, Thames and Hudson, 1992)

Macey, David
The Penguin Dictionary of Critical Theory
(London and New York, Penguin Books, 2001)

Therborn, Göran
The world: A Beginner's Guide
(Cambridge and Malden, MA, Polity Press, 2011)

Weber, Max
The Protestant Ethic and the Spirit of Capitalism
(London and New York, Routledge, 2001)

PICTURE CREDITS

Picture credits are listed alphabetically by the name of the architect or architecture firm, where applicable. Every reasonable attempt has been made to identify owners of copyright. Errors and omissions notified to the Publisher will be corrected in subsequent editions.

INTRODUCTION

George Coles p17 James Pallister

Le Corbusier p9 Bettmann/CORBIS

Durham Cathedral p10 Edwin Smith / RIBA Library Photographs Collection

Free Presbyterian Church p13tl Allan Maciver

Hagia Sophia p8 David Medd / RIBA Library Photographs Collection

Tom Greenall and Jordan Hodgson p15 Image courtesy of the architect

Andrea Palladio p13tr RIBA Library Photographs Collection

Joseph Paxton p12 RIBA Library Books & Periodicals Collection

SANAA p16 Dean Kaufman

Basil Spence p7 Eric de Maré / RIBA Library Books & Periodicals Collection

PROJECTS

Luis Aldrete pp202–207 All photography courtesy of Paco Perez Arriaga; All drawings courtesy of the architect

Andrea Dragoni Architetto + Francesco Pes pp154–159 All photography courtesy of ORCH Alessandro Chemollo except for p155 Massimo Marini; All drawings courtesy of the architect

Shigeru Ban p14 and pp22–27 All photography courtesy of Steven Goodenough; All drawings courtesy of the architect

Bayer & Strobel Architekten pp166, 167, 170, 171, 172 (b) and 173 (b) courtesy of Peter Strobel; pp168, 172 (t) and 173 (t) courtesy of Christian Koehler; All drawings courtesy of the architect

Bernardo Bader Architekten pp148, 150 (b), 152 (t) and 153 courtesy of Adolf Bereuter; pp149 and 153 (b) courtesy of the architect; pp150 (t) and 152 (b) courtesy of Marc Lins; All drawings courtesy of the architect

Beton pp34–39 All photography courtesy of the architect; All drawings courtesy of the architect

BNKR Arquitectura pp184–189 All photography courtesy of Esteban Suárez; All drawings courtesy of the architect

bureau SLA pp86–91 All photography courtesy of Jereon Musch; All drawings courtesy of the architect

Kashef Chowdhury | URBANA pp68–73 All photography courtesy of Kashef Mahboob Chowdury; All drawings courtesy of the architect

Claus van Wageningen Architecten pp120–125 All photography courtesy of Christian Richters except for p123bl Kim Zwarts; All drawings courtesy of the architect

Itami Jun Architects pp92–97 All photography courtesy of Shinichi Sato; All drawings courtesy of the architect

Jun Aoki & Associates pp80–85 All photography courtesy of Daici Ano; All drawings courtesy of the architect

Katsuhiro Miyamoto & Associates pp196–201 All photography courtesy of Takumi Ota; All drawings courtesy of the architect

Mancini Enterprises pp174–179 All photography courtesy of Niels Schönfelder; All drawings courtesy of the architect

Nómena Arquitectos + Ximena Alvarez pp40–45 All photography courtesy of Juan Solano; All drawings courtesy of the architect

O Studio Architects pp46–51 All photography courtesy of Iwan Baan; All drawings courtesy of the architect

Office for Peripheral Architecture pp28–33 and pp214–221 All photography courtesy of Jussi Tiainen; All drawings courtesy of the architect

Otxotorena Arquitectos pp52–57 All photography courtesy of Pedro Pegenaute; All drawings courtesy of the architect

John Pawson pp74–79 All photography courtesy of Gilbert McCarragher; All drawings courtesy of the architect

Randić Turato pp190–195 All photography courtesy of Robert Les; All drawings courtesy of the architect

Stanley Saitowitz | Natoma Architects pp108–113 All photography courtesy of Rien van Rijthoven; All drawings courtesy of the architect

SeARCH pp132–137 All photography courtesy of Iwan Baan; All drawings courtesy of the architect

studio tamassociati pp143–144 courtesy of Marcello Bonfanti; pp142 and 145–147 courtesy of Studio Tamassociati, Raul Pantaleo; All drawings courtesy of the architect

Toyo Ito & Associates, Architects pp62–67 All photography and drawings courtesy of the architect

+udeb arquitectos pp115–116 Sergio Gómez; p117t Gerardo Olave Triana; p114, p117b, pp118–119 courtesy of the architect

Undurruga Devés Arquitectos pp209, 211 and 213 (b) courtesy of Cristóbal Palma; pp208, 210 (t), 212, 213 (t) courtesy of Sergio Pirrone; All drawings courtesy of the architect

Wandel Hoefer Lorch Architekten pp102–107 All photography courtesy of Roland Halbe; All drawings courtesy of the architect

Kris Yao | Artech pp160–165 All photography courtesy of Jeffrey Cheng; All drawings courtesy of the architect

Peter Zumthor pp126–131 All photography courtesy of Hélène Binet; All drawings courtesy of the architect

INDEX

Author Acknowledgements
Thanks to all of the participating architects,
and to all my editors, past and present. Special
mentions to Virginia McLeod and Elizabeth
Clinton at Phaidon, Shahed Saleem at Makes-
pace Architects, Lesley Hutcheson, Nick Hayes,
Andrew Robert MacDowall, Lesley and Roger
Read, Matt and Joanna Pallister, Nicola and
Ottilie Pallister-Read.

Phaidon Press Limited
Regent's Wharf
All Saints Street
London N1 9PA

Phaidon Press Inc.
65 Bleecker Street
New York, NY 1001

www.phaidon.com

First published 2015
© 2015 Phaidon Press Limited

ISBN 978 0 7148 6895 0

Commissioning Editor: Emilia Terragni
Project Editors: Tom Wright, Virginia McLeod
Editorial Assistant: Elizabeth Clinton
Production Controller: Leonie Kellman

Design: Basedesign
Matías Aros, Marc Panero

Printed in China